VINTAGE

LIVING
TEXTS

THE ESSENTIAL
GUIDE TO
CONTEMPORARY
LITERATURE

Martin Amis

SERIES EDITORS
Jonathan Noakes
and
Margaret Reynolds

Also available in Vintage Living Texts

Margaret Atwood

Louis de Bernières

Sebastian Faulks

Ian McEwan

Toni Morrison

Salman Rushdie

Jeanette Winterson

VINTAGE
LIVING
TEXTS

Martin Amis

THE ESSENTIAL GUIDE
TO CONTEMPORARY
LITERATURE

The Rachel Papers
London Fields
Time's Arrow
Experience

VINTAGE

Published by Vintage 2003

2 4 6 8 10 9 7 5 3 1

First published in Great Britain in 2003 by Vintage
Random House, 20 Vauxhall Bridge Road,
London SW1V 2SA

Random House Australia (Pty) Limited
20 Alfred Street, Milsons Point, Sydney,
New South Wales 2061, Australia

Random House New Zealand Limited
18 Poland Road, Glenfield,
Auckland 10, New Zealand

Random House (Pty) Limited
Endulini, 5A Jubilee Road, Parktown 2193, South Africa

The Random House Group Limited Reg. No. 954009
www.randomhouse.co.uk

A CIP catalogue record for this book is available from the British Library

ISBN 0 0994 3765 1

Papers used by Random House are natural, recyclable products made
from wood grown in sustainable forests; the manufacturing processes
conform to the environmental regulations of the country of origin.

Typeset by Palimpsest Book Production Limited, Polmont, Stirlingshire

Printed and bound in Great Britain by
Bookmarque Ltd, Croydon, Surrey

While every effort has been made to obtain permission from owners of
copyright material reproduced herein, the publishers would like to apologise for
any omissions and will be pleased to incorporate missing acknowledgements
in any future editions.

CONTENTS

V

Time's Arrow

Experience

VINTAGE LIVING TEXTS: REFERENCE

Acknowledgements

We owe grateful thanks to all at Random House. Most of all our debt is to Caroline Michel and her team at Vintage – especially Marcella Edwards, Ali Reynolds, Jason Arthur and Liz Foley – who have given us generous and unfailing support. Thanks also to Philippa Brewster and Georgina Capel, Michael Meredith, Angela Leighton, Harriet Marland, Louisa Joyner, to all our colleagues, and to our partners and families. We would also like to thank the teachers and students at schools and colleges around the country who have taken part in our trialling process, and who have responded so readily and warmly to our requests for advice. And finally, our thanks to Martin Amis for his work without whom . . . without which . . .

VINTAGE LIVING TEXTS

Preface

About this series

Vintage Living Texts: The Essential Guide to Contemporary Literature is a new concept in reading guides. Our aim is to provide readers of all kinds with an intelligent and accessible introduction to key works of contemporary literature. Each guide suggests techniques for reading important contemporary novels, and offers a variety of back-up materials that will give you ways into the text – without ever telling you what to think.

Content

All the books reproduce an extensive interview with the author, conducted exclusively for this series. This is not to say that we believe that the author's word is law. Of course it isn't. Once his or her book has gone out into the world he or she becomes simply yet another – if singularly competent – reader. This series recognises that an author's contribution may be valuable, and intriguing, but it puts the reader in control.

Every title in the series is author-focused and covers at

least three of their novels, along with relevant biographical, bibliographical, contextual and comparative material.

How to use this series

In the reading guides that make up the core of each book you will see that you are asked to do two things. One comes from the text; that is, we suggest what you should focus on, whether it's a theme, the language or the narrative method. The other concentrates on your own response. We want you to think about how you are reading and what skills you are bringing to bear in doing that reading. So this part is very much about you, the reader.

The point is that there are many ways of responding to a text. You could concentrate on the methods you might use to compare this text with others. In that case, look for the sections headed 'Compare'. Or you might want to do something more individual, and analyse how you are reacting to a text and what it means to you, in which case, pick out the approaches labelled 'Imagine' or 'Ask Yourself'.

Of course, it may well be that you are reading these texts for an examination. In that case you will have to go for the more traditional methods of literary criticism and look for the responses that tell you to 'Discuss' or 'Analyse'. Whichever level you (or your students) are at, you will find that there is something here for everyone. However, we're not suggesting that you stick solely to the approaches we offer, or that you tackle all of the exercises laid out here. Choose whatever most interests you, or whatever best suits your purposes.

Who are these books for?

Students will find that these guides are like a good teacher. They introduce the life and work of the author, set each novel in its context, explain key ideas and literary critical terms as they arise, suggest comparative exercises in a number of media, and ask focused questions to encourage a well-informed, analytical approach to reading the novels in a way that is rigorous, but still entertaining.

Teachers will find in this series a rich source of ideas for teaching contemporary novels and their contexts, particularly at AS, A and undergraduate levels. The exercises on each text have been tailored to meet the various assessment objectives laid down in the subject criteria for GCE AS and GCE A Level English Literature, and are explained in such a way that they can easily be selected and fitted into a lesson plan. Given the diversity of ways in which the awarding bodies have devised their specifications to meet these assessment objectives, a wide range of exercises is offered. We've had fun devising the plans, and we hope they'll be fun for you when you come to teach and learn with them.

And if you are neither a teacher nor a student of contemporary literature, but someone reading for your own pleasure? Well, if you've ever wanted someone to introduce you to a novelist's work in a way that will let you trust your own judgement and read more confidently, then this guide is also for you.

Whoever you are, we hope that you will enjoy using these books and that they will send you back to the novels to find new pleasures.

All page references to *The Rachel Papers* and *Time's Arrow* in this text refer to the paperback Penguin editions. Page references to *London Fields* and *Experience* refer to the Vintage editions.

Martin Amis

Introduction

There are many important things to be said about Martin Amis and his work, but the first is this: that he is a great writer and his work will survive. There are reasons for this: instinct, intelligence, love of words, a commitment to form, what we can only describe as an 'eye' and an 'ear'. Amis sees, and Amis listens, never stops listening, to himself and to others.

It may be that one of the reasons why he is a great writer is because he thinks and feels about writing all the time. This is the remarkable thing about Amis – and that includes the person, the persona and the oeuvre. If you look at the interview with Amis included here, you will see what we mean. Amis is not so much a writer explaining his own work, as a highly intelligent and articulate reader examining good work with a dispassionate and a compassionate eye, and with a critical vocabulary capable of relaying that view and interpretation. Whether he's talking about voice, or method, about how the mood of a time is reflected in the works of an era, or about characterisation or narrative patterning, clear sight, clearly communicated, is always apparent.

When Frank Kermode reviewed Amis's collection of essays and reviews *The War Against Cliché: Essays and Reviews 1971–2000*

(Vintage, London, 2002) he described Amis as 'a literary critic of startling power . . . Often being right and being funny are, in this book, aspects of the same sentence'. If you want to see Amis the critic at work, it would be a good idea to read that collection.

Interestingly the double role that Amis plays, being both writer-creator and critic-reader, comes out in the patterns of his novels as well. If you look at the interview (on pp. 12–13) with Amis you will see that he speaks about the revisions that he made to *The Rachel Papers*, his first book; this was, he explains, the only time he submitted to 'editorial advice'. The advice was about the time scheme: each chapter, as you will see, begins with a reference to the eve of Charles Highway's twentieth birthday. Then, in the continuation of the chapter, he picks up the story of his youth and the writing of 'The Rachel Papers' from the perspective of the older (if not wiser) Charles.

Though Amis may never again have attended to an editor, this piece of advice was taken over and again. In *London Fields* each Chapter falls into two parts, the first section consisting of the novel Samson Young is writing, the second section being an account of how he is writing it and his interaction with the 'real life' people who are being made into his fictional characters. In *Experience* doubleness is similarly exploited. Each chapter begins in an apparently haphazard, but actually highly contrived, stream of consciousness and each chapter of Part One ends with a letter – a purportedly real letter – written by the younger Amis from school or college.

The layering of selves and time, and the layering of fiction over the 'real', parallels Amis's persistent double perspective. He writes and he analyses. He feels and he thinks. He creates and he criticises.

It can sound schematic: certainly it is contrived, for Amis is a self-confessed stylist. Even the briefest conversation with

Amis will include extended metaphors, similes, puns, analogies and a sophisticated awareness of how language works. He never stops thinking about language. He never stops tuning the instrument.

That's the technical side, but it's one that contributes to his commitment to writing and to the intensity of the experience of reading an Amis novel. The other side of his particular quality is achieved by the fact that he is always analysing, honing and discriminating, thought, feeling, consciousness, experience. He feels, examines his feeling, never letting up his attention to working out distinctions of emotions as he makes connections or discerns discontinuities. It's subtle, precise, relentlessly demanding and distinctive. If there sometimes seems a hardness, a grubbiness even, in Amis's subjects and style, there is also no waste, no flab and no sentimentality. His work will make you think. It may also make you cry.

In *Experience* Amis relates the occasion when he had an argument with his father, Kingsley Amis, about Vladimir Nabokov's famous – and infamous – novel *Lolita*. Martin admired it, Kingsley deplored it as 'thoroughly bad in both senses: bad as a work of art, that is, and morally bad'. Martin Amis tells how he tackled his father over this, quoting sentences which, he believed, were 'beautiful, dreadful, flinching and groaning with pain and grief' and which show us 'the moral soul of the entire enterprise'. He goes on to tell us that his father's reaction was: '"That's just flimflam, diversionary stuff to make you think he cares. That's just style". Whereas I would argue that style *is* morality: morality detailed, configured, intensified. It's not in the mere narrative arrangement of good and bad that morality makes itself felt. It can be there in every sentence' (pp. 120–121).

It is a quintessentially Martin Amis statement: 'style *is* morality'. And if one were to apply this statement to Amis's own work, the most obvious place to locate it may be in a reading of *Time's Arrow*. The propriety of using an elaborate and contrived literary method in relating a subject so distressing and obscene as the horrors of Auschwitz is one that Amis had to deal with carefully. It may be useful to refer to the interview (on pp. 20–21 and p. 24) to see how Amis discusses this. But, as he says, the separation of style and subject is not one that should be acceptable in literature. In fact, the method leads directly to a moral point. If time works forward (in the normal way) then the Odilo we first meet would be young, innocent of the crimes he will commit. Because time works backward, he has already committed those crimes, but because we don't know it, we – the readers – judge him only on what is presented to us at the beginning of the novel in the story of his old age. Once we discover the extent of his crimes, we are forced to reassess our own reactions, and our relation to the whole question of guilt, complicity and punishment. A serious moral proposition if ever there was one, but one brought about specifically because of Amis's stylistic method.

Reading over Amis's work – with its glittery and relentless insistence on style, and its concomitant demands made on the thinking, analysing, feeling capacity of the reader – one might begin to wonder if it is this very highmindedness that some critics cannot take, even though his adherents love it.

Reviewers don't always know what to do with Amis's work, which often leads to oddly diverse opinions. When *Experience* was published in 2000, Graham Hassell, writing in *What's on in London*, complimented the book on its 'brilliantly original' structure, as 'a quasi-autobiographical valedictory to his old dad'. Yet William Sutcliffe wrote in the *Independent on Sunday* that 'despite the insistence of his blurb-writer that this is an autobiography, Amis is curiously reticent about himself and his life. Four hundred pages of this "autobiography" somehow go by without us ever learning very much about who Martin Amis is, or what he has done with the past 51 years of his life'. You could be forgiven for wondering if they were reading the same book. Other reviewers argued over the elements that seemed to be personal when they were essentially literary, or rather acutely literary-critical. It may be true, as Amis says, that the memoir was designed to 'settle scores' with the fourth estate of hostile critics and reviewers, but that does not undermine the intellectual interest which Amis can bring to examining his own condition.

In *Experience* Amis speaks ruefully about this fact – 'my teeth made headlines' he says – but the very way in which he says this is a testimony to his writerly skills. The juxtaposition of 'head' and 'teeth', the pun in 'headlines', the simplicity, the judicious rightness, the wit – all of these exemplify the skills that make Amis into a first-class writer.

Amis has had a struggle with his critics. He struggles because he does take his work very seriously, as he takes fiction and words and literary language seriously. It's a lot to demand of the reader, but Amis intends to make demands on his audience and is unabashed about that. You have to work hard, there's no doubt about it, but the reward is a word-hoard pleasure on every page, and the sophisticated and yet compassionate encouragement to take on the examined life, as Amis himself takes it on.

Amis writes fiction because it gives him 'control'. He speaks about this craving in *Experience*:

> The trouble with life (the novelist will feel) is its amorphousness, its ridiculous fluidity. Look at it: thinly plotted, largely themeless, sentimental and ineluctably trite. The dialogue is poor, or at least violently uneven. The twists are either predictable or sensationalist. And it's always the same beginning;

and the same ending . . . My organisational principles, therefore, derive from an inner urgency, and
from the novelist's addiction to seeing parallels and
making connections. (p. 7)

The comfort in the control offered by parallels and connections does not last long. A few pages further on and he says:

Over the Christmas of 1973, experience – in the
form, as I now see it, of an acquaintance with infi-
nite fear – entered my life and took up residence in
my unconscious mind. This happenstance has shown
me, through long retrospect, that even fiction is
uncontrollable. You may think you control it. You
may feel you control it. You don't. (p. 36)

It's another doubleness. The effort to shape, set against the
acknowledgement that there will be no shape. Amis's enterprise – in his fiction, and in his attention to the processes of
his fiction – is one that admits all risk, and yet, paradoxically,
is all the safer, all the more secure for admitting that risk. In
an interview published around the time of the publication of
Experience he said:

The work at the desk was enjoyable, even though it
was emotional. The emotion still stands, rich and
good, even though painful. You're never over these
things. I did do a lot of concentrated mourning, so
I've gone a distance down the road. It's an endless
road, but I have gone quite a distance . . . There
may be a second volume eventually.

In fact, it doesn't matter whether or not there is a second
volume of memoirs. For there will always be more volumes

10

where the risk is taken, the feeling felt then ordered, the process of life into art exposed, as Amis goes on with his transfiguring.

Interview with Martin Amis

London: 10 July 2002

JN: I'm going to start by asking you about *The Rachel Papers*. I was intrigued by that line in *Experience* where you say, 'In 1973 my life looked good on paper, where, in fact, almost all of it was being lived.' How far then, in 1973, were you actually creating your voice, your career, in the process of writing this story?

MA: I think with a first novel you just have a go, with the courage and folly of youth. You get going and see how you do. I had a sense that I wouldn't just write one novel, and in fact by 1973 I was well into my second novel. I'd finished *The Rachel Papers* early in 1972. It was a long time in production, and it was the only novel of mine that was significantly rewritten on the advice of the editor. So I was conscious of being there for the long haul – put it that way – but I wasn't career building. I didn't have any kind of overview.

JN: In what ways was it rewritten?

MA: Well, it has a kind of double-time scheme, in that in each chapter you see the narrator on the eve of his twentieth birthday. And my typescript when I handed it in was not consistent then, in that some chapters just ran on, and the editor tightened it up with this suggestion, and improved it by a good fifteen per cent.

JN: Fifteen per cent! That sounds very precise . . .

MA: Well, that's what it felt like, and it's the only time that I submitted to editorial advice, and I could tell she was right straight away. So there was some tinkering going on with that, but I was already completely preoccupied with my second novel, and you're always wanting to move forward and not go back to what feels done.

JN: This very brittle, sardonic tone that is Charles Highway's voice . . . is that your own voice?

MA: You haven't got much else except your own consciousness, and I've always felt my own books are very good and dutiful examples of this. Because the first novel is about me, my consciousness; the second is about a peer group; the third is about a city; the fourth and fifth compare one city to another, New York and London; then, by *London Fields*, I'm writing about the planet, and by the time you get to *The Information* then it's the universe; and my present novel is a bit about alternate universes. So there is a steady expansion here. But when you're twenty-one, unless you're very exceptionally empathetic, you're really trapped inside your own consciousness, and what you do, and tend to go on doing, is you take a little bit of yourself and push it very much to the forefront, and all the other facets of your character are suppressed, partly for ironic effect, and it has a stylising effect too. No, the only claim that *The Rachel Papers* has to originality is that it's not 'the portrait of the artist as a young man', it's more the 'portrait of the literary critic as a young man'. I made him much colder than I am, and also he's an anti-creative figure, he's a pedant, a nineteen-year-old pedant. But even when it came to *Money*, where I had a debauched first-person narrator, I still took that two percent of me. And what you hope is that everyone has a bit of that in them, and then the novel can claim to some kind of universality.

JN: *The Rachel Papers* does feel like a young person's book, I suppose partly because of that literary critical element of Charles always teasing ideas through literature. And there's that moment when he's advised to start resorting to his own self.

MA: Well, yes, he's a chameleon and a ventriloquist. Like most people of that age, they're trying on voices and personalities and don't have much idea who they really are, and I think that's a condition of being that age. You've got to pretend an easy and urbane acquaintance with the main currents of life without knowing anything whatever, so it's all a desperate bluff, being nineteen.

JN: There's something that goes through all your books, and that's the playing with words, the extended metaphor. For example, there's a bit at the beginning of *Experience* where you're having a conversation with Louis in the car, but then you get into a whole word-play about 'the Chauffeuring Years' and the 'autobahn' of life. Is that something that happens just because you like words, or is it something that you map out for yourself?

MA: It's all instinct. When anyone asks you 'Why did you decide in this novel to have . . . ?', the word 'decide' is always wrong. You grope around your own instincts and move forward reflexively rather than to a plan. Anthony Burgess years ago made the distinction between what he calls the 'A-type novel' and the 'B-type novel'. The 'A-type novel' being characterised by a strong narrative, characters, human interest; the 'B novel' being more an order of words. The ultimate 'B novel' is [James Joyce's] *Finnegans Wake*. And most literary writers are somewhere between the 'A' and the 'B', and I suppose I lean a bit more towards the 'B'.

JN: Is there a problem – perhaps this is particular to *The Rachel Papers* – with being *so* articulate that it's not commensurate with the lack of maturity in a young person? That one can *say* things, but not feel them?

MA: That's very much Charles Highway's problem in *The Rachel Papers*. As he says – if I can remember this, I haven't looked at the novel in a quarter of a century – but something like 'having a vocabulary more refined than your emotions'. The emotions have to catch up with the vocabulary. But I would again claim that that is part of the condition of being that age. I wrote the novel feeling that I'd better get it down quickly because I'll soon forget what being nineteen is like, and it's such a volatile state that you don't really know where you're headed. You're in flux, you don't know what your destination is, you don't know what you've got in the way of talents and capacity for concentration, etc., it's a roller-coaster ride. So I thought 'quick', while it's still fresh in the memory, and I knew I was going to be a different person in a year or two. I instinctively knew that, so that was another reason for haste.

JN: I'm thinking now of *London Fields*. Having the *writer* so much in the forefront, and yet then dealing with the characters, it's almost as though you're always working on two levels, with a double perspective. And actually the way you're speaking about that now seems almost to give that double perspective

– that you're living it, and you know you've got to get it down now, but at the same time you're outside it.

MA: Yes. Well, it's a dual, it's a divided kind of process. But that's also the case with postmodern novels up to a point. People talk about postmodernism as they do all developments, evolutionary developments, in the novel, as if they were fashions or bandwagons. But when a lot of writers start doing the same kind of thing, it isn't fashion, it's the novel making another lurch forward in its evolutionary path. You can tell when this is happening when a very hard-working, though not necessarily sophisticated, fiction reviewer starts saying things like, 'Can we please have a moratorium on novels about science. I'm fed up with all these novels about science', as if it were a fad. But in fact it's not. You know something's up then, when a lot of writers are doing the same thing. And that's what we were doing *then*. And postmodernism – I always thought it was kind of a dead end, as it's proved to be, but I thought there were comic possibilities in postmodernism that I hadn't seen exploited much. By the way, I'm being wise after the event here, because you wouldn't think it through like that. So in the novel *Money* I have a character called 'Martin Amis' who has long discussions with his protagonist, John Self, and gives him great hints about what he has in store for him because he is, after all, in a godlike position vis-à-vis his main character. But of course my main character is never listening. He's always worrying about his car, or his girlfriend. And I thought *there* was a vein of comedy that was characteristically, essentially postmodern. But I don't feel I'm in that stream any more. I think we're all moving on from that kind of playful, tricksy work. It's like the architecture that has all its innards on the outside – you show the reader what you're doing. I know it was tremendously irritating to many an earlier generation, and when my father tried to read *Money* – whose first chapter he'd liked – when in the second chapter he came to the character called Martin Amis, he hurled the book across the room because by his lights it was a trick – he used to call it 'buggering the reader about' – and his idea was that it was a much straighter deal with the reader, and you didn't try and stretch or trick or puzzle the reader. But I didn't agree with him ... Now I feel that that's been done and has proved to be something of a dead end, although a theory or an idea with tremendous predictive power, because life became very postmodern, politics became postmodern. Politicians would tell you what they were doing. This was a sort of spin, I suppose, but with a self-consciousness, and an end of the old and more actorly and hypocritical political style.

JN: You're couching this very much in terms of literature, and literary forms, but is there a world spirit which dictates the fact that everybody is interested in a particular method or a particular theme at a particular time?

MA: Oh yes, and if asked to sum up the subject of literary fiction in a couple of words, I would say, 'It's about the near future.' It is about the *Zeitgeist* and human evolution, particularly of consciousness, as well as furniture and surroundings. It's how the typical rhythms of the thought of human beings are developing.

JN: Set against that, though, there is the fact that it is a *physical* existence that we lead, and in all the novels is this interest in the body, how it works. There is that intriguing statement in *The Rachel Papers* about the existence of the body giving rise to the existence of irony.

MA: Yes, it is a clunking reminder of our physical existence. Another way of putting it is that we write about a parallel track through time. We write about change, planetary change, changes in consciousness, but also about our own ageing, which has a unique unprecedented affinity with the ageing of the planet because a seventeenth-century novelist or eighteenth-century novelist would have no more sense of the planet getting older, than would the dog at his or her feet ... It wasn't in their consciousness. But now we do very much have a sense of finite time, vis-à-vis the planet. So those parallel tracks – getting older, while you write about the same things, which I think, for instance, describes the career of Graham Greene quite exactly – those preoccupations don't change, but the writer gets older as he writes about them. That track, that awareness of age is a great subject, and now I'm fifty-two I think it hasn't been done. Some writers have of course done it brilliantly, but you never do take the advice of literature on these matters. It's only when it happens to you that it feels like a completely fresh experience, as if no one gave you any warning whatever, because it's so much more immediate to feel it than to read about it. But ageing is a terrifying business that seems to have been hedged by a conspiracy of silence, once you get to it. No one would tell you it was going to be like *this*. So I look forward to chronicling that particular part as well.

JN: *London Field*: – you say in *Experience* that you thought about calling that *Time's Arrow* – or are you just playing with the reader, are you buggering the reader about?

MA: No, no. I did – the phrase was in my mind, and I didn't know that a whole novel was going to earn that title much more thoroughly than *London Fields* did.

JN: So why did the phrase 'Time's Arrow' stay with you?

MA: I don't know. I'd been reading popular science, and reading about the arrow of time, and I'd been interested in that, and it's not a totally fanciful notion to turn back, to reverse the arrow of time, because certain theories now exploded about the fate of the universe include this idea of the big crunch when everything has been flung out by the big bang, but then the explosive force of that thrust weakens, and then gravity starts to pull everything back in. And many physicists have theorised about the possibility of time going backwards in that event, and light going backwards too. But a philosopher of science friend said to me, 'Don't get into that, that's a can of worms for you. Just imagine it as a film going backwards.'

JN: How difficult – technically – was that to do? After all, you even try and do the language backwards at one point.

MA: Yes, right at the beginning. But I realised that that would have to be stylised very quickly – only a few bleats of backward speak are allowed. And then I just simply reversed the order of people saying things.

JN: But even the conversations ...

MA: Yes. The conversations are backwards in time, although each particular utterance is given as it were forward in time as a convention, otherwise the novel would have been impossible to read or write.

JN: So running the film backwards, that was the method, that was what you had in mind?

MA: Yes. I thought it was going to be a short story, a poetic short story of four or five pages, of a life done backwards.

And I'd toyed with it in a short story where I'd just done a paragraph like that. But then I thought that, even as a short story, there's not very much point to this. It's a conceit, and a beautiful and sad, tragic conceit. But then I read *The Nazi Doctors* by my friend Robert J. Lifton, and I thought, now, there would be a point. And I thought a long short story, then I thought a novella, and it became, in the end, a short novel.

JN: To juxtapose something which is tricksy and witty from a literary point of view with a huge ...

MA: ... historical tragedy ... Yes, but I mean I still think I have something to say, and the subtitle of that novel is 'The Nature of the Offence'. And what I'm saying is that the Holocaust would have been exactly what the Nazis said it was – i.e., a biomedical initiative for the cleansing of Germany – if, and only if, the arrow of time ran the other way. That's how fundamental the error was. And I think the novel expresses that. Nazism was a biomedical vision to excise the cancer of Jewry. To turn it into something that *creates* Jewry is a respectable irony. People who say that you can't use sophisticated means to speak about the Holocaust ... you know, you can only go near the subject in a sepulchral hush. With the Holocaust, it's a respectable position. Cynthia Ozick has my respect, as does George Steiner for saying that actually you can't write about it. But those who automatically think that sophisticated and witty or ironic means for writing about something serious ... that that's something impermissible, [that] is just a humour-lessness in another guise. You cannot take away your sense of humour. To excise that reduces you. Humour and common sense – as Clive James once said, 'Humour is just common sense dancing'. And those who have no humour have no common sense either, and shouldn't be trusted with anything.

JN: To my mind, it's a way of reversing orders. There's that moment when Odilo says, 'Creation is easy' – and it's brilliant because it does mean that, going backwards, people come out of Auschwitz whole . . .

MA: . . . and are then placed in ghettos and concentration camps, and then distributed among the population, and employment is found for them, and all the Nuremberg laws are reversed so they get their pets back, and their radios back. It seems philanthropic, if and only if, the arrow of time is reversed, and that's the most fundamental law of the universe . . . that it can't be.

JN: The fact that we don't know what crimes have been committed by the protagonist, because of time going backwards, puts the reader in a very curious position in relation to that character.

MA: The reader has to do all the morality, because these terrible events are described as benevolent, but also in such a way that, I hope, there is a sort of disgust and an unreality and self-delusion in the way it's shown. He keeps wondering why it has to be so ugly, this essentially benevolent action, why it is so filthy and ugly. It was a coprocentric universe. They called Auschwitz 'anus mundi'. So it's there, but the narrator can't spot it, the *reader* has to do all that.

JN: You end it with that little piece in the acknowledgements saying thank you to your sister Sally for giving you your earliest memory. What function does memory have in that work or any of the others?

MA: I don't think I rely upon it as much as some writers – Nabokov, Ian McEwan. Nabokov says explicitly that your childhood is your treasure chest as a writer. I can't say I find myself feeling that often. But when I wrote *Experience* you find that the memories are there, and unearthing them is like developing your muscles, and it gets stronger the more you do it. I think it's all there, but unconscious, it's all in the unconscious with me.

JN: Obviously in *Experience* you are drawing on memories as well as fictions and stories. Once or twice when I've taught it, funnily enough, I find myself calling it a novel . . .

MA: Ah, well, I think that's not a bad instinct. I knew when I started it that I couldn't possibly write a conventional A to B chronological memoir. I never contemplated that. Again, this is not a decision, but a decision that's already made for you. I knew I'd have to have some novelistic freedoms – the ability to jump around in time and also to follow themes rather than merely the calendar. So it's very much a memoir by a novelist.

JN: The opening conversation sets up many different things. It's about creation, because so many other stories are being brought into being with this conversation between a son and a father, or two sons and two fathers . . .

MA: Well, a writer's life is going to be peculiar. Writers' lives are usually fairly chaotic, despite what Flaubert said. You know, the writer should be orderly and boring in his life so that he can be savage and original in his work. But writers' lives do tend to be a bit savage and a bit original. But you are also placed, as everyone else is placed. You have your parents and you have your children and that is universal. So there is an Everyman, as well as a literary curiosity in every writer.

JN: You talk about reading in terms of writing something and then reading it back. How far is that the double perspective that you're often using: you are both – both the reader and the writer?

MA: You're always the reader and the writer. Writing a memoir is different. You are very much less free. Writing fiction is one of the great human expressions of freedom. You're freer than a poet because of form. You are infinitely freer than a dramatist because you don't rely on actors and props and stages and audiences and all the rest. But when you're writing about your life, you can be a galley slave, if you're actually doing it chronologically. And I wanted some authorial freedom. But when you're writing a novel, absolutely anything in it can happen. You have no restrictions of budget. You can bring about a holocaust, you can turn back the arrow of time, you have godlike powers which you never have over your own life.

JN: You begin *Experience* with a chapter headed 'My missing . . .'. How much is presence and absence a theme?

MA: What was shocking to me was finding out about my subconscious, which is where it all comes from anyway. The novelist Maureen Freely wrote a piece that really shocked me where she said that – this was on the occasion of my meeting my grown-up daughter, whom I didn't meet until she was nineteen – and Maureen Freely said that, 'in all his fiction, all his novels, there are these lost girls whose paternity or origin is in doubt'. And I suddenly realised that I had been thinking about her, and about my cousin who was murdered. That they had been very present, not in my conscious mind, but in my unconscious mind, and therefore in my fiction.

JN: Talking for a moment, not specifically about your cousin, but about Auschwitz . . . do you think it is the role of the intellectual to think about atrocities, to tackle difficult things that perhaps the survivors of such experiences can't?

MA: I wouldn't say that they can't. Primo Levi disproves that, as do many first-person accounts of these things. You don't, you shouldn't go there if you don't want to go there, but I think it would be unusual for a writer placed as we now are at the beginning of this new century not to be interested in extreme human behaviour. It's one of the great mysteries, isn't it? The enormous band of human behaviour – that we can produce a Shakespeare and a Hitler. You do not see such contrasts in the animal kingdom. You can't say, 'This is an absolutely superlative baboon, while this is a highly regrettable baboon.' They're all much of a muchness, aren't they? Human beings effloresce in incredibly different directions and degrees, and I don't see how you could fail to be interested in that. It's all telling you what it is to be human, and that is the subject.

JN: You spoke at one point about the novelist's addiction to parallels, and to making connections. Would that be a fair description of the novel as a form?

MA: Yes. I think *Experience* might give the reader the impression that every time something happens to you, you say, 'Oh, this is just like that bit in . . . Saul Bellow, or Joyce or something.' But while you are living it, you don't actually have time to make those connections. You're trying to make sense of it after the event, and you reach for similar analogous experiences, or representations of those experiences in literature. But sure, when you're writing a novel you're trying to make everything hang together. When you start a novel you're assigning life to these propositions in a kind of reckless way, and when you actually have to write the novel you're trying to control it, and it feels like an inseparable mass of many things. It's like scaling a mountain with various lines. You need themes, you need glutinations of ideas and images that control this mass.

JN: There's a way in which your perception of 'experience', the word, has changed a lot, thinking from *The Rachel Papers* through to *Experience*. It begins as something for which the characters are greedy, and it ends as something which is almost harm . . .

MA: The other side of it is innocence. I said to a journalist that innocence seemed to me to be the primary value in my fiction, that's what I value most. And he said, 'Yes, but you always write about experience, not innocence.' And I agreed.

JN: Perhaps it's not possible to know innocence unless you're experienced enough to be able to analyse it?

MA: Or innocence is a kind of *tabula rasa* on which is piled, stacked, over the years, experience, in the Blakeian sense of being more and more aware of your fallen state . . . man's fallen state, which is all nonsense theologically, and so on, but is a good enough image for our condition.

JN: You talked about your father complaining about the way that you were treating the reader. Do you have an ideal reader in mind? Because you demand quite a lot of your readers.

MA: I suppose I do. Well, I think one shouldn't pussyfoot, and just say that you write the stuff that you would like to read. So you write for yourself, no doubt about that. But I do have a sort of romantic idea of someone in their twenties, of a certain bent, and when they pick up a book by me, they think – as I have done on several occasions – 'Ah, here is one for me. Here is a writer who I'll have to read all of, because they're speaking directly to me, and they're writing what I want to read.' And sometimes you're doing the signing queue and a reader comes past and you sign the book, and there's a little exchange of the eyes, where you think, 'Ah, that's one of them.' So there is that ideal reader. And it's someone who's discovering literature and homes in on you. I'm aware of such readers.

JN: Who are the authors who you turn to, about whom you have that feeling?

MA: Well, Nabokov and Bellow are the ones where I really thought, 'That's it, and I'm going to get all their books.' And I've read every word they ever wrote. They have to be contemporary writers. You don't pick up Henry Fielding and think, 'This is one for me.' It has to be the shared experience, the shared century at least.

The Rachel Papers

IN CLOSE-UP

Reading guides for

THE RACHEL PAPERS

BEFORE YOU BEGIN TO READ . . .
— Read the interview with Amis. You will see there that he
identifies a number of themes:

● Narrative structure
● Time and memory
● The idea of the author
● Figurative language
● Youth
● The human body

Another theme that may be useful to consider while reading
the novel is:

● Relations between men and women

While you are reading *The Rachel Papers*, *London Fields*, *Time's
Arrow* and *Experience* in detail it is worth bearing these overall
themes in mind. At the end of the detailed reading section you
will find suggested contexts which will help you to situate the
themes in a wider framework.

The reading plans given below are designed to be used imaginatively. Choose whichever sections most interest you or are most useful for your own purposes. The questions which are set at the end of each chapter analysis are to help you relate each individual chapter to the novel as a whole.

Reading activities: detailed analysis

CONTENTS

Look at the Contents page. What does this list indicate about how the narrative is ordered? Each heading has two elements: the first is a time, a countdown from seven o'clock to midnight. The second suggests a journey, literal or metaphorical. What do the stages on that journey suggest? Note that 'The Rachel Papers' are within *The Rachel Papers*, but are not the whole of the novel. What does 'right Charlie' call to mind? 'Celia shits'? 'the dog days'? The point of arrival is 'coming of age'. What does this metaphor mean?

CHAPTER ONE

SEVEN O'CLOCK: OXFORD
SECTION 1 (pp. 7–8)

Focus on: openings and narrative voice

DISTINGUISH BETWEEN THE NARRATOR AND THE AUTHOR . . .
— The novel is written in the first person: that is, the narrator

is a character. Amis recalls in *Experience* that an early reviewer of *The Rachel Papers* assumed that this voice was Amis's own, and failed to see the irony, the 'stylisation', in the narrative voice. In a 'first-person' narrative, the narrator's voice is a part of his or her characterisation, and the reader 'reads' not just what the narrator says but also how s/he says it: the tone, the language, the idiosyncrasies of thought portrayed (or betrayed) by the language. The question arises of how far we can trust this narrator. You need to stay alert to any hints that the narrator may be partial, blinkered or intentionally dishonest. Look at what Amis says about narrative voice in the interview on pp. 13–14.

ASSESS WITH CLOSE READING . . .

— Read from the opening to the bottom of page 8. What impressions do you form of the narrator, Charles Highway? Attend not only to what he tells you, but also how he tells it: the language he uses, the allusions, the tone of voice. What are your first reactions to this character?

— Is this opening apparently 'spoken' or 'written'? What clues are there in the novel's title or in the narrative itself? Does it read like an interior monologue, or like spontaneous speech, or as something more self-consciously polished and performed? Pick out phrases that give indications of how this opening should be read, or understood.

COMPARE . . .

— Compare this opening, and the effects created, with other first-person narratives from various periods. You might look, for example, at the openings of Defoe's *Moll Flanders* (1722), Swift's *Gulliver's Travels* (1726), Dickens's *Great Expectations* (1860–1), Salinger's *The Catcher in the Rye* (1951), Fowles's *The Collector* (1963), or Atwood's *The Handmaid's Tale* (1986).

CHAPTER ONE
SECTION 2 (pp. 9–10)

Focus on: characterisation

ANALYSE BY DISCRIMINATING . . .
— How are Highway's mother and father presented here? Separate 'fact' from 'opinion' in his portrayals of them. What seems to be Highway's attitude to each of them?

CHAPTER ONE
SECTION 3 (pp. 11–14)

Focus on: literary allusions

RESEARCH ALLUSIONS . . .
— Highway says that he had 'that week read a selection of D. H. Lawrence's essays' (p. 11). What is the significance of this allusion? Read a selection of D. H. Lawrence's essays, such as 'The Education of the People' (1918, 1920), 'The Social Basis of Consciousness' (1927) and 'À Propos of Lady Chatterley's Lover' (1930). You might also like to look at the references to D. H. Lawrence in Amis's *Experience*. Is Amis being ironic at Highway's expense?
— 'it's just that he constitutes such a puny objective correlative' (p. 11). Look up the phrase 'objective correlative' in the glossary of literary terms. Who invented the term, and with reference to which work of art? What does it suggest about Highway's turn of mind that he applies this literary term to his father? To understand the effect of the allusion more fully, look at how Highway documents his relatives as 'characters' in his files (p. 12), and look at his attitude to his parents' sexuality (pp. 12–13). If you know Shakespeare's play

Hamlet, consider the effect of Highway's indirect allusion to it.

Looking over Chapter One

QUESTIONS FOR DISCUSSION OR ESSAYS

1. 'Charles Highway presents himself as clever and knowing, but despite himself he also betrays his limitations.' Discuss with reference to the first part of *The Rachel Papers*.

2. How is 'family' presented in these opening pages?

CHAPTER TWO

SEVEN TWENTY: LONDON
SECTION 1 (pp. 15–17)

Focus on: narrative technique

CONSIDER THE EFFECTS . . .
Evidently, there is a double-time scheme in the novel: the period of three months (September to December), during which the events that Highway is describing took place; and the period of five hours (7 p.m. to midnight) in the narrative 'present', during which he reviews his written notes on his experiences during those months. So the experiences described have been mediated twice by Highway: when he turned his original experiences into written documents, 'The Rachel Papers' and 'Conquests and Techniques: a Synthesis'; and when he reviews those documents.
— Consider how this narrative technique contributes to the theme of the relationship between life and literature, and to the theme of narrative 'self-consciousness'.

CHAPTER TWO
SECTION 2 (pp. 17–21)

Focus on: telling stories

ASSESS THE EFFECTS . . .
— The whole narrative is a story Highway is telling, and telling for obvious effects: to amuse, to shock, to satirise. What effects are created in this section, and how does Highway create them?

CHAPTER TWO
SECTION 3 (pp. 21–2)

Focus on: characterisation

CONSIDER THE USE OF SATIRE . . .
— If you are not already familiar with literary satire, look up 'satire' in the glossary of literary terms. Highway's first descriptions of his parents (pp. 12–13) focused on their physical appearances; here (pp. 21–2), he focuses on their social attitudes. What human weaknesses is Highway mocking in these two passages?

CHAPTER TWO
SECTION 4 (pp. 22–5)

Focus on: attitudes to the human body

ANALYSE . . .
— What does it say about Highway's character that he keeps a folder called 'Conquest and Techniques: a Synthesis'? What attitudes to sex are conveyed in this section?

Looking over Chapter Two

QUESTIONS FOR DISCUSSION OR ESSAYS

1.   Discuss the satirical effects created in Chapter Two of *The Rachel Papers*. Consider both Highway's satirical presentation of other characters and Amis's satire of Highway.

2.   'Writing about experience is a way of trying to control it.' To what extent does this statement apply to Highway's narrative?

CHAPTER THREE

QUARTER TO EIGHT: THE COSTA BRAVA
SECTION 1 (pp. 26–8)

Focus on: Highway's attitude to women

LIST AND ASSESS . . .
— List all the phrases that Highway uses to describe women in this section. What attitudes do these phrases convey? In your opinion does Highway betray these attitudes unknowingly, or does he intentionally highlight them?

COMPARE . . .
—'the reechiness of the bed' (p. 27). 'Reechy' is an unusual, archaic word, meaning 'dirty' or 'soiled'. Highway has already made several allusions to Shakespeare, and his use of this word in this context might allude to Hamlet's attack on his mother for living 'In the rank sweat of an enseaméd bed, / Stewed in corruption, honeying and making love / Over the nasty sty' (Act 3, Scene 4,) – in the same scene he refers to Claudius's 'reechy kisses'. Compare the language that Hamlet uses to

describe women and sex in this particular scene with Highway's language in this section.

CHAPTER THREE
SECTION 2 (pp. 28–37)

Focus on: comedy

ANALYSE . . .
— How does Amis create comedy in Highway's description of his attempts to 'pull' Rachel on pp. 32–5 and 36–7?

LOOK FOR A PATTERN . . .
— Highway stereotypes himself as 'bookish teenager' in this section (p. 35). What does he mean and how does he present himself as 'bookish' in this section?

CHAPTER THREE
SECTION 3 (pp. 37–43)

Focus on: characterisation

COMPARE AND DISCRIMINATE . . .
— Highway describes two episodes that involve Norman on pp. 37–41 and 41–3. The stereotype character that emerges from the first story contrasts with the more complex character portrayed in the second. Compare his portrayals in these two stories, and consider the effect of their juxtaposition in Highway's narrative.

INTERPRET . . .
— Bearing in mind that this narrative is Highway's story, and

that he shapes it to suit his purposes, consider the role Norman plays in this section. In the first story, Norman is presented in a way that throws Highway's own character into relief. In the second story, Norman's behaviour does not reflect on Highway, who is only a listener, but it does reflect on Highway's family. Interpret what Highway is implying about himself, and about his family, by the contrasts he creates with Norman's persona in each story.

CHAPTER THREE
SECTION 4 (pp. 43–53)

Focus on: creating a persona

CREATE . . .

— Highway prepares for Rachel's visit by carefully constructing a persona for himself, through his appearance, his manner and his room. He did something similar before a meeting with Gloria on p. 20. Create a description of his room that conveys your own interpretation of Highway's character in the novel so far.

Focus on: language

ANALYSE THE CONNOTATIONS . . .

— So far in his narrative, Highway has referred to sex as 'poking' (p. 17), 'fucking' (e.g., p. 36) and 'screwing' (p. 48), to which Geoffrey adds 'creaming' (p. 48). Investigate the etymology of these words – use a dictionary of slang if you have access to one. Three of these terms are metaphors. What attitudes to sex do they imply?

— Consider also how sexual terms are used in other contexts in the narrative: 'big-cocked' (p. 7), 'notch on the cock' (p. 22),

"No, cunt" (p. 38), "fuck off" (p. 40), "It's fucking *great* to hear your voice" (p. 44), "What the fuck are you talking about?" (p. 47) 'Cuntish public-school dropouts' (p. 49) and 'fucking DeForest's spiky insect head' (p. 52). In each case, the metaphor says as much about attitudes to sex as it does about the thing described. Look at the contexts of the words in each case, and analyse their connotations.

INTERPRET THE JUXTAPOSITION . . .
— After the caricature of public-school conversation on p. 50, Highway describes a similar group as 'chatting contrapuntally' (p. 50). What do you think this phrase means? What effect does Highway create by using a self-consciously recondite term to describe a clichéd conversation?

Focus on: point of view

INFER AND CREATE . . .
— Highway imagines what Rachel may be thinking of him on p. 52. Rachel's reaction to his leaving on p. 53 suggests that his fears that she despises him are unfounded. Infer from her reactions what she thinks of Highway and his advances. You could, if you wish, express her thoughts as an interior monologue.

CHAPTER THREE
SECTION 5 (pp. 53–8)

Focus on: contrasts

IDENTIFY AND COMPARE . . .
— Highway ironically describes the scene in his bedroom as 'a scene of almost pastoral spontaneity' (p. 53). Look up 'pastoral' in the glossary of literary terms if you are unfamiliar

with this literary genre. The description that follows (up to p. 58) mixes imagery that suggests harmony and nature with images that suggest distortion, violence and contamination. Identify these two types of images and consider the effects created by their combination.

ANALYSE NARRATIVE STRUCTURE . . .
— What is the effect of juxtaposing Jenny and Norman's row in the background with the scene in the foreground?

Looking over Chapter Three

QUESTIONS FOR DISCUSSION OR ESSAYS

1. How well does Highway know himself, in your opinion?

2. By referring to two episodes, analyse Highway's presentation of Norman in *The Rachel Papers*.

3. 'In *The Rachel Papers*, Highway presents sexual relations as exploitative and loveless.' Discuss, with reference to the first three chapters.

CHAPTER FOUR

THIRTY-FIVE MINUTES PAST EIGHT: THE RACHEL PAPERS, VOLUME ONE
SECTION 1 (pp. 59–64)

Focus on: the theme of life and literature

DISCUSS . . .
— What does this section contribute to the theme of the relationship between life and literature?

RESEARCH . . .

— Amis makes several references in *Experience* to the people and experiences in his own life on which *The Rachel Papers* is (at least partially) based. Refer to Amis's comments on the woman he used as a basis for Rachel on p. 264 of *Experience*, and to the model used for Mr Greenchurch (p. 342). He comments that, 'Of course, only a semiliterate would say that Harold Skimpole *is* Leigh Hunt or that Rupert Birkin *is* D. H. Lawrence; of course, even the most precisely recreated character is nonetheless *recreated*, transfigured; of course, autobiographical fiction is still fiction — an autonomous construct' (p. 226). Finally, read what Amis says about basing his story on his own experiences in the interview (on pp. 13–14). What do you conclude about Amis's view of the relationship between life and literature?

CHAPTER FOUR
SECTION 2 (pp. 64–5)

Focus on: narrative technique

IDENTIFY . . .

This episode is one of a series in which Highway refers to an 'issue' between Jenny and Norman which at the earlier time he could sense but could not understand. Highway, the narrator in the narrative 'present', *does* understand it, and will eventually disclose what is at issue between them. This technique of delayed disclosure is a form of manipulation: it elicits from the reader a parallel series of reactions to those in the characters as events unfold, from confusion and intrigue to realisation; and it implicitly emphasises the narrator's superior knowledge, his control over how much he discloses, and when.

— What aspects of Highway's character (as narrator) are emphasised by his use of delayed disclosure here?

CHAPTER FOUR
SECTION 3 (pp. 65–73)

Focus on: the theme of performance

DISCRIMINATE . . .

— Highway is a performer, both in his life and on paper. How far do his actions in this section seem to you to be 'spontaneous' (p. 65), and how far do they seem to be a 'ploy' (p. 68)? Does his claim, 'my conceit is an unmanned canoe, leaping imaginary rapids' (p. 68), add anything to your understanding of how his mind works?

CONSIDER . . .

— 'Rachel's character was about as high-powered as her syntax' (p. 72). What does this comment reveal about Highway's beliefs about articulate expression? Is his own character as high-powered as his syntax?

— 'Irony and blood returned to my features' (p. 73). In what senses can irony be said to run in Highway's veins?

RESPOND . . .

— 'How about you?' (p. 73). This is Highway's only direct challenge to the reader. Answer it.

CHAPTER FOUR
SECTION 4 (pp. 74–87)

Focus on: character

EVALUATE . . .
— In an early review of *The Rachel Papers*, Peter Prince described Highway as a 'Sixth Form Sneerer, that combination of middle-class privilege and A level meritocracy'. Evaluate the accuracy of this description with reference to this section of the novel.

Looking over Chapter Four

QUESTIONS FOR DISCUSSION OR ESSAYS
1.   'For all his intellectual precociousness, Highway's habit of interpreting his world through literature betrays an immaturity that is both emotional and intellectual.' Discuss.

2.   How accurate is the phrase 'herd-instinct sexism' in describing the attitude of the male characters to the female characters in the novel so far?

CHAPTER FIVE

NINE: THE BATHROOM
SECTION 1 (pp. 88–96)

Focus on: attitudes to the human body

EXAMINE . . .
— In the opening paragraphs of this section, Highway considers a possible connection between his fascination with physical grotesqueries and his sense of humour. He puts this down

to a 'Sound distrust of personal vanity' (p. 88), which is the underlying justification of all satire: the satirist exposes the gulf between how we like to see ourselves and the reality. Examine Highway's preoccupation with the human body in this section, and consider whether it is satirical.

— He later says that 'the existence of the body is the only excuse, the only possible reason, for the existence of irony' (p. 180). What does he mean by this? See the comparison with Swift in the Contexts section (p. 61).

CHAPTER FIVE
SECTION 2 (pp. 96–104)

Focus on: the theme of connection and separation

ANALYSE WITH CLOSE READING . . .
— Analyse Highway's description of his attempts to seduce Rachel which runs throughout this section. In what ways does this description emphasise the distance between the two characters rather than their connection? How aware of this effect is Highway?

Looking over Chapter Five

QUESTIONS FOR DISCUSSION OR ESSAYS
1. Discuss Amis's presentation of the human body in Chapter Five of *The Rachel Papers*.

2. 'The cruelty of the humour in *The Rachel Papers* is tempered by a sense of the absurd.' Discuss, with reference to Chapter Five.

CHAPTER SIX

HALF AFTER: RIGHT CHARLIE
SECTION I (pp. 105–20)

Focus on: attitudes to sex

COMMENT ON . . .
— Is Highway's attitude to his father's mistress hypocritical, in your view? Justify your answer.

Focus on: social satire

RESEARCH AND DISCUSS . . .
— The social satire of Chapter Six shares a number of features with the dramatic form called the 'comedy of manners'. If you are unfamiliar with this genre, refer to the glossary of literary terms. Discuss how Amis employs stock character types in social situations to create comedy in Chapter Six.

COMPARE . . .
— Compare the presentation of Highway's experiences in Chapter Six with the way that the hero of Kingsley Amis's *Lucky Jim* (1954) shows up his right-wing university colleagues as pretentious fools. In what ways are the two novelists' satirical techniques similar, and in what ways are they different?

Looking over Chapter Six

QUESTIONS FOR DISCUSSION OR ESSAYS
1. Consider the significance of the title of Chapter Six.

2. In what ways does Chapter Six develop Highway's characterisation?

CHAPTER SEVEN

TEN FIVE: THE SPINNEY
SECTION 1 (pp. 121–4)

Focus on: the double-time scheme

REFER AND ASSESS . . .
— Refer to what Amis says in his interview (on p. 12–13) about how he was persuaded by his editor to start each chapter with a reference to the double-time scheme – the countdown to midnight as Highway reviews the last three months of his life. An earlier draft, he says, was not consistent in doing this. What effects do these openings in the fictional present add to the narrative?

Focus on: motivation

INFER . . .
— What are Highway's motivations for the way he reacts to the school bullies? How clearly does he explain them? Do you believe the reasons he gives?

CHAPTER SEVEN
SECTION 2 (pp. 124–9)

Focus on: attitudes to gender

COMPARE . . .
— Compare Highway's comments on men and women on p. 125 with the attitudes he has displayed up to this point in the novel.

Focus on: puns

DISCUSS . . .

— 'I felt neurotically high-cheek-boned as I closed the door' (p. 126 – he has an erection) and '"Mum's the word"' (p. 127) are typical of the puns that you will have noticed pepper Highway's narrative, in that they are self-consciously playful but otherwise empty of meaning. His recurrent wordplay reminds the reader that it is Highway's brittle voice we are hearing, his hand that (so the illusion goes) is controlling the narrative of *The Rachel Papers*. Why is it important that this illusion – that the controlling hand is Highway's, not Amis's – is continually reasserted?

CHAPTER SEVEN
SECTION 3 (pp. 129–36)

Focus on: life and literature

COMPARE . . .

— The episode on pp. 129–30 recalls the scene in Shakespeare's *Romeo and Juliet* (Act 3, Scene 5) when the lovers wake up after their first night together. But this scene inverts it: Highway has not spent the night with Rachel (why?); their love is not forbidden (he is more worried about his parents knowing he smokes); it is not the birds singing, but the radiator pipes making the noise. Compare the two scenes. What effects are created by the implied comparison? What is Highway saying about the relationship of life to literature?

ANALYSE . . .

— Analyse the way that Highway recounts the episodes on pp. 130–1 and 131–3. What is he implying about the stories we

47

tell about life, and the reality? In what ways is his presentation of the 'reality' only another story?

Looking over Chapter Seven

QUESTIONS FOR DISCUSSION OR ESSAYS

1.   Highway casts a tennis match as 'that gladiatorial combat between innocence and experience' (p. 135). Consider the claim that he casts his own story in those terms throughout Chapter Seven.

2.   Discuss the relationship between 'experience' and 'writing about experience' in Chapter Seven of *The Rachel Papers*.

CHAPTER EIGHT

TWENTY-FIVE OF ELEVEN: THE LOW
SECTION 1 (pp. 137–43)

Focus on: language

GAUGE THE IRONY . . .

— Never far behind Highway's accounts of his amatory adventures are literary models against which he ironically measures his own experiences. Elaine's account of Gerry's preoccupations on p. 137 (in the paragraph starting, '"Gerry, the cat I was balling . . ."') is a neat summary of the themes of much literature about love, and in particular the themes of *Romeo and Juliet*. Look at Elaine's emotionally and linguistically clichéd, poverty-stricken way of talking about love. What ironies are set up in the implied comparison between her language and Shakespeare's?

DISCUSS . . .

On p. 8, Highway said that he was reviewing the last three months to locate his '*hamartia*', a word taken from the Greek and meaning 'error of judgement' or 'tragic flaw', specifically when applied to a hero from tragic drama. In this part (pp. 139–43), he extends his models to Shakespearean tragedy, to Romantic literature, to twentieth-century modernist and to existentialist literature, in an attempt to find significance in his experience. Yet his own 'descent into manhood . . . retrospectively seems avoidable, without significance, second-rate, not worth it' (p. 139).

— Discuss the relationship between the literary models that he uses to interpret his experiences and the experiences themselves, as he recounts them on pp. 139–43.

Looking over Chapter Eight

QUESTIONS FOR DISCUSSION OR ESSAYS

1. Highway cites the literary convention of 'the *nadir* period' to describe this stage of his story (p. 139), but this part of the novel is entitled, more prosaically, 'the Low'. Consider the significance of this title in the novel's presentation of how Highway interprets his life.

2. 'I seemed incapable of using words without stylising myself' (p. 142). Discuss, with reference to Chapter Eight.

CHAPTER NINE

ELEVEN TEN: THE RACHEL PAPERS, VOLUME TWO
SECTION I (pp. 144–59)

Focus on: life and literature

INFER . . .

—— 'My files really are in need of thorough reorganisation. A good way to spend my twentieth birthday?' (p. 144). Highway earlier described midnight on the day of his twentieth birthday as the threshold to adult experience, and claimed that his review of his papers was a way of taking stock of his adolescent self before leaving it behind. What does the question above betray about his actual motives?

CONSIDER THE IRONIES . . .

—— Read 'The Clod and the Pebble' from Blake's *Songs of Innocence and of Experience* (1794), the poem that Highway quotes from on p. 145. He claims that he quotes the poem only for effect. Does the poem have a relevance to his life that he does not recognise, or does not acknowledge? Consider the description of his seduction of Rachel that follows. Is Amis being ironic at Highway's expense, or is Highway being ironic about his own cynical motives?

—— 'that's what I'm here for tonight. I must be true to myself' (p. 149). Do you read this as a sincere statement of Highway's intent, or as another irony, another pose? How can you tell?

Focus on: language

ANALYSE AND COMPARE . . .

—— Analyse the language that Highway uses to describe sex

with Rachel on pp. 153–9. What is the significance of the allusions on p. 158 to the last part of T. S. Eliot's poem 'The Love Song of J. Alfred Prufrock'?

CHAPTER NINE
SECTION 2 (pp. 159–61)

Focus on: teeth

COMPARE . . .
— Highway has made references to his teeth throughout (e.g., on p. 29). He is not the only Amis character to suffer from poor teeth. See, for instance, John Self's obsession with his teeth in *Money* (1984). See also Amis's focus on the problems he experienced with his own teeth that runs throughout *Experience* as a kind of leitmotif, recalling the difficulties and humiliations of life. What symbolic significance might Highway's poor teeth have?

Looking over Chapter Nine

QUESTIONS FOR DISCUSSION OR ESSAYS
1. Consider the accuracy of Highway's claim that he has 'a vocabulary more refined than [his] emotions' (p. 154).

2. 'For Highway, fiction is more real than life.' Discuss.

CHAPTER TEN

TWENTY-PAST: 'CELIA SHITS' (THE DEAN OF ST PATRICK'S)
SECTION 1 (pp. 162–6)

Focus on: the title

RESEARCH AND COMPARE . . .

— The Dean of St Patrick's was the great eighteenth-century satirist Jonathan Swift. The allusion in the title is to his poem 'The Lady's Dressing Room', in which 'Disgusted *Strephon*' steals away from his peephole, 'Repeating in his amorous Fits, Oh! Celia, Celia, Celia shits!' Read this, and his other so-called 'obscene' poems, 'Strephon and Chloe', 'Cassinus and Peter' and 'A Beautiful Young Nymph Going to Bed' (all written 1730–1). What is Swift saying in these poems about beauty, love and physical reality? Do they make a satirical – i.e., a moral – point about human nature?

— Examine Highway's reference to 'My one unfallen week' (p. 164), which echoes 'prelapsarian high spirits' (p. 150). What does Highway mean by 'fall' and 'lapse'? See also his comment that only 'on the lavatory [. . .] was I possessed by a truly radical vision of life; only there did I really *feel*, in my heart, that, somehow, we were all guilty' (p. 166). What similarities can you find between Swift's attitude and Highway's?

Focus on: narrative point of view

ASSESS . . .

— 'Charles looks at the clock . . .' (p. 162). Highway has written about himself in the third person at several points in the narrative (see pp. 132–3 especially). What does this habit of casting himself as a character in his own narrative suggest about the kind of narrative this is?

CHAPTER TEN
SECTION 2 (pp. 166–77)

Focus on: sex and love

COMMENT . . .

— Look at the opening line of this section, 'After briefly wanking myself off on top of her . . .' He later describes his feelings for Rachel (on pp. 169, 171) as 'First Love', and tells her he loves her (pp. 170–1: who says it first?). But he tells Geoffrey that being with Rachel is 'Nothing special' (p. 173). Comment on Highway's attitude to Rachel. Look especially at the passage on pp. 176–7. Does any of this connect with the title of this part, 'Celia Shits'?

— Highway tries to catalogue his 'First Love' and to file it away. Why? He refers to 'fear in a handful of dust', a quotation from T. S. Eliot's *The Waste Land* which itself refers to human fear of mortality ('ashes to ashes, dust to dust'). Comment on the claim that 'Highway tries to assert intellectual control over reality because it frightens him'.

Focus on: forms of communication

INFER . . .

— Who is Highway likely to be ringing, here and on p. 162? His letter to his father was first mentioned on p. 68. It has taken him weeks, and is still undergoing revisions. He originally intended it as a speech. What is the letter likely to say, do you think, and why has he written it rather than spoken it? What parallel is there between his letter to his father and 'The Rachel Papers'?

CHAPTER TEN
SECTION 3 (pp. 177–82)

Focus on: the ideal and the real

ANALYSE . . .

— Analyse how this section contrasts notions of 'the ideal' and 'the real' (including the passage about his examinations).

CHAPTER TEN
SECTION 4 (pp. 182–90)

Focus on: delayed revelation

ASSESS . . .

— Highway the narrator has delayed revealing the 'issue' between Jenny and Norman. When Rachel tells him, he realises that she has kept it from him. What is his reaction to this realisation?

Focus on: dream narrative

INTERPRET AND CONTRAST . . .

— Interpret Highway's dream. How does the emotional logic of his dream narrative contrast with Highway's usual methods of intellectually structuring his narratives?

Looking over Chapter Ten

QUESTIONS FOR DISCUSSION OR ESSAYS

1. Discuss attitudes to the human body in Chapter Ten.

2. Consider the claim that Highway's obsession with structure and order is a reaction to 'the messiness and arbitrariness of our . . . unwanted desires' (p. 184).

3. Compare Highway and Rachel's relationship with Norman and Jenny's.

CHAPTER ELEVEN

TWENTY TO: THE DOG DAYS
SECTION 1 (pp. 191–6)

Focus on: structure

COMMENT . . .
— Highway has said earlier that, 'a structural view of things [is] always the very best view of things to take, in my opinion' (p. 173). Comment on his interview preparations in the light of this comment.

CHAPTER ELEVEN
SECTION 2 (pp. 196–202)

Focus on: comedy

ANALYSE THE NARRATIVE TECHNIQUE . . .
— How does Highway create comic effects in this section? Look for some of the traditional elements of farce: exaggerated characters and situations, absurdity, improbable events, the dominance of plot and situation over character and dialogue.

CHAPTER ELEVEN
SECTION 3 (pp. 202–4)

Focus on: deceit

ASSESS . . .

— Highway contrasts his mendacity to Rachel's on p. 203 ('With fresh curiosity . . .'). How accurate is his appraisal, do you think (bear in mind the last scene with Gloria)?

Focus on: character

REINTERPRET . . .

— In what ways does the revelation of Rachel's dishonesty cause you to alter your view of her? Who has had the controlling hand in your assessment of Rachel up to this point?

Looking over Chapter Eleven

QUESTION FOR DISCUSSION OR ESSAYS

— Examine the theme of pretence in the novel so far.

CHAPTER TWELVE

MIDNIGHT: COMING OF AGE
SECTION 1 (pp. 205–8)

Focus on: Norman

COMPARE . . .

— 'Are we all such emotional Yahoos?' (p. 207) alludes to the fourth book of Swift's *Gulliver's Travels*. Read Chapter VII of that text, from 'He was the more confirmed . . .' to the end of the chapter, in which a Houyhnhnm (a species of perfectly rational horse) compares Gulliver, a man, to the Yahoos. Is Highway any less of a Yahoo than Norman?

CHAPTER TWELVE
SECTION 2 (pp. 208–19)

Focus on: coming of age

SUMMARISE . . .
— Summarise the ways in which Dr Knowd tells Highway to grow up, intellectually.

RECONCILE . . .
— Can you reconcile Highway's loving attention to 'The Rachel Papers' with his treatment of Rachel herself?

INTERPRET . . .
— What does Highway mean by 'I wonder what sort of person I can be' (p. 219)?

EVALUATE . . .
— In what senses, if any, has Highway 'come of age' by the end of the novel?

Looking over the whole novel

QUESTIONS FOR DISCUSSION OR ESSAYS
1. 'Highway's sneering conceit is redeemed by his sense of irony.' Discuss.

2. In what ways is *The Rachel Papers* ironic at Highway's expense?

3. Discuss the use of literary allusions in *The Rachel Papers*.

4. Assess the relationship between literature and life in *The Rachel Papers*.

5. How does Amis convey the idea that Highway's capacity to feel experience does not match his capacity to articulate it?

6. Consider the significance of characters' names in *The Rachel Papers*.

7. 'The true teenager is a marooned ego' (p. 201). Discuss ideas of 'the teenager' in *The Rachel Papers*.

8. 'The novel points unflinchingly to the inadequacy of a romantic attitude towards the facts of our lives.' Discuss notions of 'the ideal' and 'the real' in *The Rachel Papers*.

9. What does Norman's character contribute to the themes of *The Rachel Papers*?

10. Analyse Highway's relationship with his father.

11. Consider the validity of the claim that 'Highway uses language not as a way of relating to others, but as a tool for controlling them'.

12. '*The Rachel Papers* makes a serious point about human nature: that we have little cause for pride.' Discuss.

13. Discuss the theme of 'experience' in *The Rachel Papers*.

14. Write an account of the events of the novel from Rachel's point of view: 'The Charles Papers'.

Contexts, comparisons and complementary readings

THE RACHEL PAPERS

These sections suggest contextual and comparative ways of reading these four texts by Amis. You can put your reading in a social, historical or literary context. You can make comparisons — again, social, literary or historical — with other texts or art works. Or you can choose complementary works (of whatever kind) — that is, art works, literary works, social reportage or facts which in some way illuminate the text by sidelights or interventions which you can make into a telling framework. Some of the suggested contexts are directly connected to the book, in that they will give you precise literary or social frames in which to situate the novel. In turn, these are either related to the period within which the novel is set, or to the time — now — when you are reading it. Some of these examples are designed to suggest books or other texts that may make useful sources for comparison (or for complementary purposes) when you are reading *The Rachel Papers*, *London Fields*, *Time's Arrow* and *Experience*. Again, they may be related to literary or critical themes, or they may be relevant to social and cultural themes current 'then' or 'now'.

Focus on: the human body in satire

COMPARE . . .

— Compare Amis's ironic attitude to the body with Swift's in Parts 1 and 2 of *Gulliver's Travels* (1726). If you haven't time to read these parts whole, look at Part 1, Chapter 2, from 'I had been for some hours' to 'to call in question' and at Part 2, Chapter 5, from 'The maids of honour often invited Glumdalclitch' to 'for not seeing that young lady any more'. Swift's attitude is essentially moral: a swipe at human vanity and pride. He presents the human body as a symbol of humanity's fallen condition, as a source of shame and disgust: the stench, the faeces, the uncleanliness of the human body are symbols of our sin.

— Then look at Highway's references to a woman he had casual sex with: 'Admittedly the girl was quite hideous, had smelled unclothed of open wounds and graveyards, etc.' (p. 45). The final image recalls that of women's bodies smelling of 'dead babies' (p. 19).

— Read over pp. 88–96 again. Look at the references to excrement in the chapter entitled 'Twenty-past: "Celia shits" (the Dean of St Patrick's)'. How do you react to these images of human physicality? Do you detect a moral repugnance like Swift's – an insistence that, whatever else we are, human beings are animals who eat, sleep, defecate and copulate, and to remember that is a salutary balance to spiritual pride? Can Amis's account of Highway's narrative be read as a moral comment on human vanity?

Focus on: physical and moral sleaziness

COMPARE . . .

— Compare Highway's physical and moral sleaziness with that

of John Self in Amis's novel *Money* (1984), a corrupt and crazed protagonist who seeks to satisfy his uncontrolled appetites for money, sex and drugs in New York, a city where he is a lunatic among lunatics.

Focus on: reliable and unreliable narrators

CONSIDER AND COMPARE . . .

— Throughout *The Rachel Papers*, Highway shapes events and personas for effect. His enjoyment of 'telling stories' calls into question how much we can trust, as the narrative contains several hints that he exaggerates. How many sexual partners has he really had, for instance? He seems remarkably uncertain in his first sexual encounter with Rachel. How should a reader react to a narrator who is possibly 'unreliable'? Of course, an unreliable narrator works only if s/he is unreliable in predictable ways, otherwise the reader will be merely confused: the narrative must give hints about when and whether to trust the narrator.

— To whom is Highway's narrative addressed? The question 'How about you?' on p. 73 suggests that his narrative is directed at a reader – it is, therefore, a performance; and a highly self-conscious one, in which even apparently telling lapses (why, for instance, was he crying on pp. 136, 138?) may not be the unguarded revelations they appear.

— Compare Highway with the narrator of Amis's novel *Success* (1978). In Part 9: September (ii) of *Success*, Riding unequivocally confesses that his narrative until that point has been riddled with lies. Do we have any more reason to trust Highway?

Focus on: the theme of coming of age

CREATE . . .

— Write your own coming-of-age narrative. Make it as long or as short as you like. Write it in the first person. Ask yourself: who is my imagined reader? How do I want to present myself? Which people shall I include? How shall I shape events for effect? How shall I finish?

COMPARE . . .

— There are many novels on the theme of coming of age. You might look at Turgenev's *Fathers and Sons* (1861); or Philip Roth's *Portnoy's Complaint* (1969), which treats the theme as farce, heavy with sex and Jewish stereotypes; or the semi-autobiographical novels of D. H. Lawrence, *Sons and Lovers* (1913), and of James Joyce, *A Portrait of the Artist as a Young Man* (1916), which describes the writer's struggle for self-expression. To compare first-person narratives in coming-of-age novels, read J. D. Salinger's comic novel *The Catcher in the Rye* (1951), a confessional, rambling monologue by a seventeen-year-old who has escaped his upbringing on the run in New York; or Jeanette Winterson's *Oranges Are Not the Only Fruit* (1985), which challenges conventional ideas about the family and sexuality; or Hanif Kureshi's *The Buddha of Suburbia* (1990), which tracks the narrator's sexual awakening and his escape from stifling suburbia.

LOOK AT POETRY . . .

— Simon Armitage's *Book of Matches* (1993) contains a section called 'Becoming of Age'. Read the poem 'To His Lost Lover'. Compare the speaker's reflections on his finished relationship with Highway's. Read also the poem 'Becoming of Age' from the section of the same title. Compare the techniques used by the speaker in this poem for locating the moment of 'becoming

63

of age' in place and time with those used by Highway in 'The Rachel Papers'.

RESEARCH AND COMPARE . . .

— The theme of 'coming of age' is one that crops up in many films about young people. Unlike a novel, however, films of this kind tend to focus on one key event or trauma which the protagonist, hero or heroine, sees as the moment of transition, when they leave behind the world of childhood innocence and ignorance and are initiated into the adult world of experience and knowledge. Examples of such films might include François Truffaut's *Les Quatre Cents Coups* (*The 400 Blows*, 1959), Peter Weir's *Picnic at Hanging Rock* (1975), John Duigan's *The Year My Voice Broke* (1987), Rob Reiner's *Stand by Me* (1986) and Terence Davies's *Distant Voices, Still Lives* (1988).

VINTAGE
LIVING
TEXTS

London Fields

IN CLOSE-UP

Reading guides for

LONDON FIELDS

BEFORE YOU BEGIN TO READ . . .
— Read the interview with Amis. You will see there that he
identifies a number of themes:

- Narrative structure
- Time and memory
- Past, present, future
- Naming
- The idea of the author
- Figurative language
- Fictionality
- Postmodernism

Other themes that may be useful to consider while reading
the novel include:

- Relations between men and women
- The depiction of violence
- The image of the city

Reading activities: detailed analysis

THE DEDICATION

Focus on: reference and connection

RESEARCH, COMPARE AND CONSIDER . . .

— Find out about Amis's father Kingsley Amis. Look him up in a biographical dictionary or in a copy of *Who Was Who*. Read one of his novels – *Lucky Jim* (1954) is perhaps the best known. You might also read Amis's own memoir called *Experience* which includes many scenes and conversations with Kingsley Amis. In what ways might Martin Amis's *London Fields* relate to Kingsley Amis's literary style, his themes, or his narrative methods?

CHAPTER HEADINGS

Focus on: patterning and play

STATE . . .

— The twenty-four chapters of *London Fields* are grouped here in five discrete sections, three chapters each for the first four, and twelve in the last section. Look at the titles given to the chapters in the first four groups. Consider how each of the titles relate to the others in their group. Then look at the last group of twelve chapters. How might you make a pattern of literary connection and reference across this larger group? Write out three sentences that describe the effects of this wordplay and thematic patterning: you should think about a) the controlling author, b) the reader's reaction, and c) the literary qualities of this method.

NOTE

CONSIDER . . .
— This Note to the reader seems to be offered to you in the voice of the author explaining how he, haphazardly, came to give his novel a title. How innocent is this Note? Or is it ironic? Consider what effect the presence of this Note has on you in creating your attitudes to a) the novel you're about to read, and b) your idea of what the novelist does and how.

INTRODUCTION (pp. 1–3)

Focus on: the idea of writing and the writer

LIST AND REFLECT . . .
— Write down all the words and phrases connected with writing and fiction in this brief introductory section. Then list all the times when the narrative goes in for some wordplay, whether it be repetition, extended connections (as in the list of kinds of sharks on p. 2), puns, or literary terms. Consider what this attention to the writing of fiction does to you as a reader as you begin to read the novel. Are you intrigued or puzzled?

ASK YOURSELF . . .

— Who do you suppose is writing here? We know that he is called Sam. Write down as many things as you can that you have learned about Sam's character from these three pages.

CHAPTER I (pp. 4–14)

THE MURDERER

Focus on: characterisation

ANALYSE AND ASSESS . . .

— We are introduced here to Keith Talent. He is not very likeable. How does the narrative persuade you to go on reading about him? How does it attempt to convey Keith's own attitudes and values without judgment? How effective is this method of creating a character? Do you think that you are expected to identify with Keith or not? How are your reactions being manipulated by the techniques of the text?

COMPARE . . .

— While the first part of Chapter I (pp. 4–9) is directly about Keith and written in the third person, the second part (pp. 10–14) is still about Keith, but written in the first person and the storyteller is the novelist Sam that we met in the first few pages. It seems also that pp. 4–9 are the novel (or true story) that Sam is writing. Compare the two sections. What difference does it make to your view of Keith to have it mediated by Sam's first-person intervention?

Focus on: *characterisation and the representation of women*

DESCRIBE AND ASK YOURSELF . . .

— Write two descriptions of Keith's girlfriend Kath. The first should be based entirely on the information you have here. With the second you should add in whatever appropriate details that you consider help to flesh out your picture. Describe her physical appearance, her attitude to Keith, her attitude to her baby, what kinds of things she likes to cook, her experience of childbirth. Then ask yourself two things: first, what is it *in the text* that allows you to make up the rest of the details about Kath's life? And second, how do you feel about the way that Kath is presented, and what do you think you are meant to feel?

Focus on: *plot*

REMEMBER . . .

— On p. 9 we are told 'Keith didn't look like a murderer. He looked like a murderer's dog.' This seems to be a straightforward observation at this point. But bear it in mind and consider these statements again once you have read to the end of the novel.

CHAPTER 2 (pp. 15–26)

THE MURDEREE

Focus on: *time*

CONSIDER AND ASSESS . . .

— Carefully read the first paragraph of this chapter (p. 15). It is written in the future tense. At the same time, though, it evokes the past 'unrecallably and for ever', and yet feels very present and immediate. Think about the ways in which this triple-time focus is achieved in this chapter. Then bear that information in mind as you carry on reading the rest of the novel. Be alert always to which scenes are set in the present, which in the past, and which in an imagined future. Be aware also of the number of times that a scene or an episode gets repeated from one point of view and then another.

Focus on: Nicola Six

THINK ABOUT SIXTH SENSE . . .

— Consider Nicola's name. If you look ahead, you will see that there is joke about it on p. 37 where Keith mishears her as she tells him her name. But why else might her surname be 'Six'? What is a 'sixth sense'? What is 'second sight'? If you read the paragraphs introducing Nicola (pp. 15–18), you will see that Nicola 'always knew what was going to happen next'. In relation to the question of time in the novel, assess how the fact of Nicola's ability to foresee the future might affect the narrative structure of the text.

CONSIDER THE ASSOCIATIONS . . .

— Go on thinking about Nicola's name. Later on, Keith will call her 'Nicky' and 'Nick' and even 'old Nick'. What associations might this suggest? Think also about Nicola's surname and where she lives. Watch out for the moments when you are told the numbers in her address, flat number and house number. Then ask yourself what associations they might bring to mind.

Focus on: fictionality

INTERPRET THE NARRATIVE METHOD . . .

— By now you might have realised that each chapter of *London Fields* has two sections. The first part is – as it were – the novel

that Sam Young is writing. The second part is his authorial
commentary on what he has written, and it also includes an
account of his own interaction with his 'characters' (assuming
that they are 'real' people). So in Chapter 2, for instance,
pp. 15–22 are 'the novel', and pp. 23–26 are the 'authorial commentary'. Consider how this might affect your own perspective
as a reader of the text. Then write down the effects that this
narrative method allows for. You might include the fact of repetition, as the story revisits a scene or episode already related;
or you might include the fact that this can offer divergent
points of view. As you read each of these 'double' chapters,
try to bear the effects of the narrative method in mind.

CHAPTER 3 (pp. 27–43)

THE FOIL

Focus on: foil, fool, foal

LOOK BACK AND COMPARE METHODS OF WORDPLAY . . .
— If you look back at p. 1 you will see that the 'author' of
this text tells us that he knows who the 'foil, the fool, the poor
foal' will be, and that he knows that he will be 'utterly destroyed'.
Now we arrive at a chapter headed 'The Foil'. Compare that
brief introduction and allusion with this more expansive
account of Guy Clinch's character and situation. As you read
on, think about the relevance of his name. (Names are never
irrelevant in Amis's work.) Think also about wordplay. It is
there in 'foil, fool, foal', but how often do you encounter it in
other places? Watch out for this technique. It might consist of
alliteration and assonance (for example on p. 29: 'softly snarling
with asthma', or 'emblazoned with eczema'), or it might consist of repetition (for example: on p. 28, 'Guy Clinch had every-

thing. In fact he had two of everything', compared with p. 29, 'So two of everything, except lips, breasts, the walls of intimacy, enfolding arms, enfolding legs').

Focus on: fictionality and the text

ASSESS . . .
— On pp. 42–3, Sam (the writer/narrator of the text as a whole) tells us that he is now in possession of something that each of his three main characters has written: i.e., Keith's brochure; Nicola's diaries; and Guy's fiction. Sam then goes on to ask himself if — as a consequence of his being in possession of these 'real' manuscripts — he is writing 'documentary' and not fiction. What do you think? Does the fact of his having these items in his possession make you believe in the authenticity of the text as a whole? Or does it make you more aware of its fictionality?

Focus on: the image of the city

LOOK AT THE LANGUAGE . . .
— Read the last three paragraphs on p. 43. Consider the language and imagery used here to describe the city. It is London being portrayed — and in the late 1980s London was the scene of a destructive tempest — but what larger images of the idea of the city are being suggested? Consider which words in this paragraph contribute to an impression of banality, and which imply more poetic qualities.

Looking over Chapters 1, 2 and 3

QUESTIONS FOR DISCUSSION OR ESSAYS
1. Why might it be relevant that our first encounter with Nicola takes place as she prepares for and attends a funeral?

2. 'Amis never creates one fiction, but two or three.' Discuss.

3. How would you describe a) Keith, b) Nicola and c) Guy? Write five sentences for each.

4. Consider how the map of the city is influencing the structure and tone of *London Fields* so far.

5. Assess the importance of descriptions of clothes in the novel so far.

CHAPTER 4 (pp. 44–64)

THE DEAD-END STREET

Focus on: double perspective

NOTE DOWN AND ASSESS . . .

— Read each of the two parts of this chapter and make out a pattern which shows the way each section of the story relates to the others. Split it up so that you have worked out how many times the narrative returns to repeat a scene or an episode, or gives you the 'before' or the 'after' to a scene. Then note down the differences between the individual depictions of the same scene or episode. These might be to do with point of view, language, things noticed and prioritised, or it might even be to do with actual stated facts. How does the 'double perspective' of the narrative affect your attitude a) to the characters, and b) to the text itself?

Focus on: authorial control

REFLECT . . .

— On p. 58 Keith hurt his thumb and 'dropped everything'. On p. 59 Sam tells us he couldn't go on with the scene and had to 'drop everything'. Think about this juxtaposition. In what two different senses is this same phrase used? What does this tell you about authorial control in the novel?

Focus on: the idea of the city

NOTE DOWN . . .

— Jot down some notes on all the descriptions of the streets or the city in this chapter. What image is building up, and what language is used to describe it?

— Then look at the last section of the chapter on p. 64. The narrator – Sam presumably – tells us that 'I want time to get on with this little piece of harmless escapism. I want time to go to London Fields.' Assess how many puns, or doublenesses of language, there might be in this last paragraph.

CHAPTER 5 (pp. 65–81)

THE EVENT HORIZON

Focus on: allusion

RESEARCH . . .

— Find out about the phrase 'event horizon', as in the chapter title. What does it mean? As you read on, consider what elements in the chapter might justify the title.

Focus on: suggestions, hints and contradictions

ASSESS AND INTERPRET . . .

— Look at the first three sections of Chapter 5. The first (pp. 65–6) focuses on a description of the flowers Keith gave to Nicola, and on Keith; the second (p. 66) is the brief story of Nicola's imaginary childhood friend Enola Gay; and the third (pp. 66–9) gives an account of Nicola's attitude and addiction to sodomy.

— Now begin by thinking about the name Enola Gay. Does it mean anything to you? If you look ahead to p. 124, you will see that when Nicola tells Guy a story about her lost friend Enola Gay there is a hint that it perhaps should mean something: 'She checked Guy's face. Nothing. And a little knowledge might have helped him here.'

— Look also at the paragraph describing Enola Gay and Little Boy (p. 66). You will need to look back at this later.

— Go on thinking about the name 'Enola'. Do you know anyone called Enola? Where do you suppose the name comes from? Then write it out backwards. What does it spell?

— Take this backwards name as a paradigm and apply the same ideas about contradiction and things being 'backward' to reassess both the first section on the flowers in this chapter (pp. 65–6) and the third (pp. 66–9).

Focus on: 'sixth sense' and the 'reliable narrator'

EXPLAIN . . .

— Several times in this chapter reference is made to Nicola's capacity for 'sixth sense' or 'second sight'. Examples might include p. 70 ('She arranged herself for Keith's visit with considerable care, despite the fact that she knew how things would go anyway, more or less'); or p. 74 ('The physiological effects of this thought told her all over again that he was the one'); or p. 75 ('It was the right car: the murderer's car').

— Explain how these allusions and reminders might relate to Sam Young's claim on p. 78, 'Man, am I a reliable narrator ...'

Focus on: language play

NOTE DOWN AND COUNT UP . . .
— On p. 81 one of Keith's acquaintances assesses Sam's national and racial origins in cockney rhyming slang. Playing games with language and vocabulary is a distinctive feature of Amis's work. Note down all the examples of this as you come across them, and then count up the different kinds of play that you encounter.

CHAPTER 6 (pp. 82–102)

THE DOORS OF DECEPTION

Focus on: numbers

PAY ATTENTION . . .
— Notice each time a number is used in this chapter. Notice also that Sam begins his second half of the chapter by telling us that Nicola 'really did a number on Guy Clinch' (p. 97). And note what he says that 'number' was. Also, what does 'duplicity' (p. 93) mean? Look it up. How might these numbers and the narrative insistence on them relate to the themes of the novel as a whole?

Focus on: telephone boxes

CONSULT YOUR OWN EXPERIENCE . . .
— Look at the passage on p. 94 about telephone boxes. Consider what telephone boxes mean to you. What do they look like, in Britain, in other countries? Why do people use

them? How do these things that you have thought of relate to the account Amis gives? *London Fields* was published in 1989. What has happened since then that means that people don't use telephone boxes as much as they once did?

Focus on: the title

ASSESS THE RELEVANCE . . .
— On p. 95 we are told 'On Sunday he had walked with Nicola Six in London fields'. Bear in mind the title of the novel and keep coming back to consider the relevance and significance of the title each time 'London fields' is mentioned. Create a list of these instances.

AND REMEMBER . . .
— We were told in the author's 'Note' that he had considered the possibility of calling this novel 'Time's Arrow'. Look at p. 88 where we are told about Guy, 'But he wasn't about to stray. He was a straight arrow.' As you read on, think about arrows – and darts – and time and other images that might have made 'Time's Arrow' a suitable title. You might create a list of such episodes.

Focus on: allusion

COMPARE . . .
— On p. 101 there is a reference to a book by Saul Bellow called *More Die of Heartbreak*. Amis cites Bellow as one of the writers who most influenced him. Read *More Die of Heartbreak* by Bellow and relate it to this passage and to the novel as a whole. You might also look up the poem by W. B. Yeats mentioned here and consider how it connects to the themes of *London Fields*.

Looking over Chapters 4, 5 and 6

QUESTIONS FOR DISCUSSION OR ESSAYS

1.   Consider the implications of the theme of dress and dressing up in the novel so far.

2.   Discuss the theme of 'sending love back the other way' in relation to this section and to the novel as a whole.

3.   'Keith Talent is a brilliant comic creation.' Do you agree?

CHAPTER 7 (pp. 103–20)

CHEATING

Focus on: language play

EXPLAIN . . .

— On p. 105 Keith and Kath have a conversation about the news. We are also given baby Kim's interjections. Strictly speaking, these aren't words, only sounds. But they do make a pattern of words. Think about each of the 'words' Kim says. How might you relate them to the themes of the novel as a whole?

Focus on: fictionality

ASSESS . . .

— Look at the passage on pp. 117–20 where the 'author' of the story, Samson Young, decides to consult Nicola on the planning of his plot. What is the effect of this intervention in the narrative by a character? Look also at the interview with Amis where he speaks about his father complaining that he was 'buggering the reader about' (on pp. 16–17). What is your own attitude to this device? Do you feel betrayed? Puzzled? Involved? Complicit? Intrigued?

CHAPTER 8 (pp. 121–38)

GOING OUT WITH GOD

Focus on: allusion and reference

RESEARCH AND CONSIDER . . .

— There are a great number of allusions to other texts in this chapter. Note them down as you read. Look especially at the list on p. 121, but you will see many others. How many of them do you recognise straight away? How many of them do you have to look up? Note down quotations as well as names of authors, books, poems, and historical and fictional characters. If you recognise them, what is the effect? If you don't recognise them, does it matter? How much information are you able to glean from the context here?

Focus on: clichés and dead metaphors

EXAMINE . . .

— When Nicola begins the story of Enola Gay, as she tells it to Guy, the text uses a number of phrases that have become shorthand for suffering, for instance: the orphanage, Cambodia, concentration camp, 'the charity school (cum blacking factory)', the farming out to 'a pitiless Iraqi'. Can you assign a context to each one of these? If you can't pinpoint a particular historical setting or a particular story, let your imagination seek out something. Think – for instance – about Charlotte Brontë's *Jane Eyre* (1847) in relation to 'the charity school', or

about Charles Dickens's life, and his novel *David Copperfield* (1849–50) in relation to the 'blacking factory'.
— Then compare this method of reference in Nicola's story to the paragraph on p. 125 where Guy gives Nicola an account of the state of his heart. What is the effect of this casual appropriation, firstly of the recognisable terms of suffering, and then of a list of clichés which include the word 'heart'? How cynical is the literary method being used here?

Focus on: plot

LOOK BACK . . .
— Read Nicola's story to Guy about Enola Gay and Little Boy, and turn back to p. 66, where we met Enola Gay before, to refresh your memory about this aspect of the story.

Focus on: word games

REACT TO . . .
— 'On its door was a white sign bearing red letters: DANGEROUS STRUCTURE. This was her body. This was her plan' (p. 129). Think about this. How does it work? What does it mean? When you have read further, think about it again.

CHAPTER 9 (pp. 139–63)

DOING REAL GOOD

Focus on: vocabulary and wordplay

LIST AND COMPARE . . .
— Keith lists the kinds of sexual encounters he has known (p. 154). How many different words does Amis give him? If you have been keeping a note of examples of this kind of

virtuosity of vocabulary in the novel, add these examples to your list. How many more could you adduce? Use a thesaurus, once you've exhausted your own imagination. What is the literary effect of these lists?

Focus on: plot and fictionality

ASSESS YOUR OWN REACTION AND REMEMBER . . .
— Sam and Nicola have another conversation about how the plot will go (pp. 161–2). Look at all the references here to radiation and energy construction. If you don't know what the words and terms mean, look them up. Keep this information for later.
— Why are the professors in Nicola's faked letter called 'Barnes' and 'Noble' (p. 162)? It refers to an American business; you might like to look it up on the internet. What do you think of the way in which Nicola is manipulating Guy?

Looking over Chapters 7, 8 and 9

QUESTIONS FOR DISCUSSION OR ESSAYS
1. How do the chapter headings here relate to a) each other, b) the content of each chapter, and c) the themes of the book as a whole?

2. 'Packed with allusion, you need to bring a lifetime's reading to reading Martin Amis.' Do you agree?

3. How and with what literary means is the character of Nicola Six constructed?

4. What is the purpose of Kim Talent's role in *London Fields*?

5. 'Boy, am I a reliable narrator' (p. 162). Do you agree?

CHAPTER 10 (pp. 164–85)

THE BOOKS IN KEITH TALENT'S APARTMENT

Focus on: literary reference

PLAY . . .

— Try and work out all the literary allusions in this chapter. What was the title of the book that Nicola gave to Keith? Check out pp. 145 and 164 for the clues.

— Then also make a list of all the allusions to literary genres and methods. For instance, on p. 167, 'When it came to kissing and telling, Keith was a one-man oral tradition.' What form of publication do you associate with 'kiss and tell'? And what is the 'oral tradition'? Also note every reference to books and to reading. What is the cumulative effect of these pointers?

Focus on: the double structure of the novel

NOTE . . .

— You will have become used to the double method of each chapter – the first section as part of Sam's novel, the second as his account of his life and his composition process. Note also how many scenes are repeated, usually twice, but sometimes three times, from different points of view or including different information.

— On p. 176 Nicola tells Keith to tell something to Guy, but we aren't told what it is. Later on we will be. That in itself is a repetition. Look out for the moment when we learn what it is.

CHAPTER II (pp. 186–210)

THE CONCORDANCE OF
NICOLA SIX'S KISSES

Focus on: lists

ASSESS THE METHOD . . .

— Nicola's kissing techniques are listed (pp. 186–7). What is a concordance? Is this an appropriate term in this case? If not, why not? How does the term 'Concordance' used in the chapter title relate to words used in the other two chapter titles in this section?

Focus on: the theme of time

NOTE . . .

— 'For the last time' is a phrase used often in this chapter. How is time being used here? Consider it especially in relation to the 'fact' that Nicola knows that she is soon to die and is measuring out the remains of her time.

Focus on: repetitions

COMPARE . . .

— Read pp. 15, 192 and 465 where the passage beginning 'The black cab' appears each time. (If you don't want to have the ending of the novel – partly perhaps – revealed to you, then skip this exercise.) Note down the similarities between these three repeated scenes, and note down the differences. What conclusions do you draw from your comparison?

Focus on: fictionality

ASK YOURSELF . . .

— Mark Asprey has the initials MA (p. 205). So does Marius

Appleby. Why do you think this is? What does it suggest to you?

CHAPTER 12 (pp. 211–41)

THE SCRIPT FOLLOWED BY GUY CLINCH

Focus on: stories and storytelling

NOTE DOWN AND COMPARE . . .

— In the course of this chapter several characters either tell stories to themselves (like Guy's fantasy about what will happen with Nicola when he finds Enola Gay, p. 215), or they tell stories to each other (like the tale of the blind man crossing the road, pp. 221–2). Ask yourself how this relates to the themes of the novel as a whole.

— Then look at these lines in the 'Sam's life' half of the chapter: 'I called Guy and told him not to do anything rash while I'm away' (p. 234); 'Keith himself of course I couldn't do anything about' (p. 234); ' "I couldn't ask you, could I, Nicola," I said on the phone, "to be prudent, and keep activity to the minimum while I'm gone?" ' (p. 235).

— How does Sam attempting to take control of his story – and his characters – connect to the other stories told in this chapter?

Focus on: doubleness

CONTEMPLATE . . .

— The chapter structure changes after Chapter 12. Instead of the groups of three as set out so far, we have one section consisting of twelve chapters. Sam the 'author' of the story also goes away here, and then returns. Consider again all the range of 'doublenesses' you can think of that describe and frame the literary method and the themes of the novel as a whole.

Looking over Chapter 10, 11 and 12

QUESTIONS FOR DISCUSSION OR ESSAYS

1. 'Toys were symbols – of real things' (p. 220). Discuss, in relation to this section of the novel.

2. Compare and contrast the two babies in the novel, Marmaduke Clinch and Kim Talent.

3. Consider the ways in which Amis plays with names and naming in this section and in the novel as a whole.

CHAPTER 13 (pp. 242–63)

LITTLE DID THEY KNOW

Focus on: the body

DISCRIMINATE AND ASSESS . . .

— Begin by considering the ways in which Marmaduke's skin condition is described on pp. 243–5. Think especially about words like 'jewelled' (p. 243), 'fantasticated' (p. 243), or the comparison with 'Io, Jupiter's molten moon' (p. 244). Using this close reading as a basis, look over the rest of the chapter to compile a picture of how the body is presented in this text. Then consult the interview with Amis where you will see that he talks about his attitudes to the body and the facts of our physical existence (on pp. 17–18). How far do these attitudes inform and colour the text as a whole?

Focus on: typologies

RESEARCH, RELATE AND COMPARE . . .
— On p. 260 Sam is trying to find an archetypal description to fit Nicola and he says, 'I love these typologies.' What is a typology? Look it up if you don't know. How does this connect to the various lists of words and icons that Amis has been using throughout the novel?

Focus on: language and wordplay

LOOK BACK . . .
— If you turn back to p. 105, you will recall the passage where baby Kim's interjections made up a subtext to a conversation between Keith and Kath. On p. 256 you will find another example. Compare the two passages, and again consider Kim's words and how they apply to this section and to the themes of the novel as a whole.

CHAPTER 14 (pp. 264–84)

THE PINCHING GAME

Focus on: The Pinching Game

RELATE . . .
— 'What was she doing?': on p. 258 we don't know the answer and Keith does not know the answer. Here (p. 264) we learn the answer. Look at this and then look at the description of the rationale and method of 'the pinching game' (p. 279). How might the game be a fair description of the method of the novel?

CHAPTER 15 (pp. 285–305)

PURE INSTINCT

Focus on: black humour and double entendre

ASK YOURSELF IF IT'S FUNNY . . .

— Nicola carries on seducing Guy. Keith (and Sam, and Amis) work on his predicament with *double entendre*s. On p. 292, for example, Keith is talking about a parking space, but implying something else: 'Was it okay, asked Keith, if he *took his place*. He'd nip in where Guy'd just been' etc. Think about why this might be funny. And think about why Nicola's manipulation of Guy comes across as funny — even when it's potentially disastrous for Guy himself. Can you point to elements in the language and the phrases used that diffuse the seriousness of these situations?

Focus on: the theme of love and death

THINK . . .

— A long reverie about death — the word and the fact — and about love occurs on pp. 296–7. Read it through carefully. How many other common phrases can you think of with the word 'death' in them? And with the word 'love' in them? Compare your two lists. How far are the sentiments and attitudes similar, and how far are they different? Think about your own attitudes to death, and to love. What do you imagine each to be? What is your own experience of each? In what ways might they relate to each other?

Focus on: The Pinching Game

LOOK AGAIN . . .

— Nicola and Sam use the image of the Pinching Game in

their discussion on pp. 304–5. Look back at the first time we were introduced to this game (p. 274 and p. 279) and assess this new reference.

CHAPTER 16 (pp. 306–327)

THE THIRD PARTY

Focus on: vocabulary

NOTE AND CONNECT . . .
— Keith scatters his conversation with references to engine and car vocabularies (pp. 306–7). He resorts to nonsense phrases and assonances (p. 308). Then he's given a virtuoso language of darts performance (pp. 312–14). How might these extravaganzas connect to the others you have read in the course of the novel and the themes of the novel as a whole?

Focus on: London Fields

COLLECT REFERENCES . . .
— 'I must go to London Fields, before it's too late' (p. 323). If you've not already begun to do so, start noting down each time 'London Fields' is mentioned. When you have a complete list, having read to the end of the book, see how this pattern of reference illuminates the plot and the themes of the novel.

CHAPTER 17 (pp. 328–50)

CUPID'S COLLEGE

Focus on: romance

COMPARE . . .

— Examine the ways in which romance and the language of romance are used in the section. Which words and phrases remind you of popular romances like Mills & Boon novels or sentimental films?

— Then seek out all the references to the poems of John Keats in this chapter. They start at p. 342 where Nicola tells Guy that she is teaching Keith about English literature. But there are at least two other references on p. 344. How might Keats's poetic language differ from the popular language of romance?

Focus on: literary criticism

ASK YOURSELF . . .

— Why is it appropriate to the themes and concerns of the novel as a whole that Nicola should pretend to be teaching Keith how to read literature?

Focus on: value

CONSULT YOUR OWN OPINION . . .

— Incarnacion goes on at Sam about the ashtray and the lighter (p. 350). She distinguishes between 'face value' and 'sentimental value'. What do these terms mean to you? What objects have 'sentimental value' for you? Why do we value objects? Write a list of the possible reasons. How might the question of 'values' and what we 'value' be relevant to the novel as a whole?

CHAPTER 18 (pp. 351–70)

THIS IS ONLY A TEST

Focus on: joke histories

COMPARE . . .

— Keith reads his history of darts to discover that Boadicea played a form of darts in AD 61 (p. 351). Look back over the chapters you have read so far to find the other passages where Keith consults his history of the game of darts. Obviously this is all rubbish – or is it? But why is it amusing? Compare Amis's joke about the history of darts with other well-known perversions and distortions of the facts of history. You might like to read W. C. Sellar and R. J. Yeatman's *1066 and All That* (1930), or to watch *Monty Python's Life of Brian* (1979). How do these joke histories work on us, and how are they 'double'?

Focus on: joke histories and Keats

ASSESS . . .

— What do you think of Nicola's Keats lesson (pp. 352–6)? You might want to look at some of the poems that Keith and Nicola are supposed to be criticising here and work out your own opinions. In what ways is there a connection between what Nicola is doing, and the joke histories that you've been thinking about?

RESEARCH . . .

— Keith imagines a book called *Keith and Embarrassment*. There is a real critical book on the poet called *Keats and Embarrassment* by Christopher Ricks (1974). Amis obviously knows the book as this allusion appears here. How might the methods of the critic have influenced the methods of Amis the writer?

— Look at the interview with Amis. How often does he cast

93

himself there in the role of the literary critic? What might that tell you about his techniques and interests in general?

Focus on: the theme of love

LOOK BACK AND COMPARE . . .
— A passage on p. 367 has Sam playing with terms that have the word 'love' in them. Look back at the section on pp. 296–7 where love is also discussed. Compare the two passages.

Focus on: double meanings

THINK ABOUT . . .
— Sam reads what Keith has written: '*Got to stop hurting K. No good just takeing it out on the Baby*' (p. 370). What do you understand this to mean? Might it have more than one meaning? Remember it – you will need to come back to these sentences later.

CHAPTER 19 (pp. 371–91)

THE LADIES AND THE GENTS

Focus on: darts and time's arrow

LOOK THROUGH AND CONSIDER . . .
— Read the account of the events at the darts match carefully. You will remember that Amis said in his Note that he had thought of calling the novel 'Time's Arrow'. What elements in this episode would have made that a suitable title?

Focus on: Enola Gay

NOTE . . .
— Why do you suppose Nicola asks Paul Go if the name 'Enola Gay' means anything to him (p. 379)?

Focus on: Nicola Six

THINK ABOUT NAMES . . .
— Nicola's name – whether first name or surname – is mentioned on pp. 386, 403 and 404. What do these references add to your understanding of the significance of her name?

Focus on: literary criticism

RESEARCH AND INTERPRET . . .
— Nicola gives Guy 'a series of literary kisses' (p. 384). Try to locate where these characters are from. In which texts do Maud, Geraldine, Eve and Ophelia appear? When you've found out about them, consider the ways in which they might be like, or unlike, Nicola as a character.
— Then read the passage on pp. 388–91 where Sam and Nicola discuss his plotting and what she – as a character in his novel – can and cannot do. How does the fact of Nicola discussing her own characterisation and impact on the plot affect your attitude to her as a literary character?

Focus on: Kim Talent

NOTICE . . .
— Look back to p. 370 where Sam reads what Keith has written: '*Got to stop hurting K. No good just takeing it out on the Baby.*' Now Sam visits Kim and discovers her wounds (pp. 387–8). Remember this episode for later.

Focus on: vocabulary

LOOK UP . . .
— Nicola smiles an 'exalted' and 'veridical' smile (p. 390). Look up 'veridical' in a dictionary. What does it mean? Why does Amis — or Sam — use it here?

CHAPTER 20 (pp. 392–412)

PLAYING NERVOUS

Focus on: 'who loved nobody'

SPECULATE . . .
— We are told that Richard 'loved nobody' (p. 394). Then we are told that Nicola 'loved nobody' (p. 395). Why might they be linked in this way? How does 'loving nobody' illuminate the themes of the novel?

Focus on: joke histories

ADD TO YOUR LIST . . .
— Keith reads another excerpt from his history of darts (p. 396). Add this to your list of examples of this kind of episode. When you get to the end of the novel read all the excerpts from the darts history together and consider how they might function as a commentary on the action of the novel as a whole.

Focus on: dolorology

LOOK UP . . .
— What does 'dolorology' mean (p. 408)? Look it up in a dictionary. In what ways might this be compared with the typolo-

gies, concordances, lists and thesauruses that you have encountered so far in the novel?

CHAPTER 21 (pp. 413–36)

AT THE SPEED OF LOVE

Focus on: London Fields

NOTE DOWN . . .
— There is another reference to 'London Fields' on p. 416. If you are still noting down each time it is mentioned, add this to your list. Why is this particular mention of the name slightly different from ones that have gone before – and that will come after?

Focus on: allusion and reference

RESEARCH . . .
— '"It's nothing to do with the office," he kept telling a Mr Tulkinghorn' (p. 418). Mr Tulkinghorn is a character in a novel by Charles Dickens. Try to find out which novel, and find out about the character, and then consider why this allusion might be appropriate.

Focus on: surprise

ASK YOURSELF . . .
— Think about brothers in this novel. Where are they? Bear this in mind for later. Remember that 'doubleness' and reflection is a theme throughout.

Focus on: parentheses

NOTICE AND WORK OUT WHY . . .
— Why does '(Keith)' keep appearing in brackets or parentheses in the passage on pp. 420–1? What is the literary effect of this stylistic device?

Focus on: Kim Talent and Kath

EXPLAIN . . .
— ' "I'm a wicked woman, Sam," ' says Kath (p. 436). What do you think she means?

CHAPTER 22 (pp. 437–55)

HORRORDAY

Focus on: horror

CONSIDER THE IMPLICATIONS . . .
— Look back at p. 426 where Nicola gives Keith one of her home videos and says it's on a 'Halloween theme'. He replies, 'Horror like?'
— First, ask yourself what 'Halloween' means. If you don't know, ask someone or look it up. What might be the *opposite* of the term? (Remember that much of *London Fields* works on oppositions and doubles.) Does it work as 'Horrorday'?
— Now read Chapter 22 and carefully note all the words that have acquired the prefix 'horror'. What do you make of this device? Why is it there? What does it do to you as a reader?

Focus on: allusion and reference

RESEARCH AND ASSESS . . .
— Look up the Shakespeare sonnet that Nicola has copied into the book she has given to Guy for his return journey (p. 441). Think about the meaning of the poem. Then assess a) how this poem is an appropriate choice in the light of Nicola's machinations, and b) how the themes of the sonnet might be relevant to the themes of Amis's novel.

Focus on: Kim Talent

THINK ABOUT . . .
— Consider what you are told on p. 454 about Kim's injuries. Given that you have been noting the references to the passage of Keith's writing that Sam reads on p. 370, are you surprised at this, or not? How can you connect this revelation to the themes of the novel as a whole?

CHAPTER 23 (pp. 456–63)

YOU'RE GOING BACK WITH ME

Focus on: the chapter title

IMAGINE . . .
— Later on in this chapter you will find a passage that directly explains the title of this chapter. But think about this phrase now. Imagine what it might mean. Think about how it might apply to the novel as a whole.

Focus on: time and repetition

MAKE CONNECTIONS AND EXAMINE DISTINCTIONS . . .
— This chapter opens with a repetition. Look back at p. 15.
What words are the same? What words are different?

Focus on: point of view

COMPARE . . .
— Nicola says, '"Do you think this dress is sufficiently
disgusting?"' (p. 455). Sam says, '"Oh, wear a coat, Nicola"'
(p. 455), and his narrator (presumably) says, 'Disgustingly attired
(how *could* she?)' (p. 456). But on p. 458 we are told that Keith
'had never seen her looking quite so beautiful'. Compare their
points of view. What does this tell you about the attitudes typ-
ified by these four perspectives?

Focus on: brothers and London Fields

RELATE TO . . .
— 'I must go back to London Fields . . . I played there with
my brother as a child. So long ago' (p. 463). Explain the
metaphoric significance of the reference to London Fields, and
of the reference to Sam's brother. (You might look ahead here
to p. 469 for a clue. Or else, make a note to check back over
this section when you get there.)

CHAPTER 24 (pp. 464–7)

THE DEADLINE

Focus on: the chapter title

ANALYSE IN CONTEXT . . .

— What does this chapter title mean? Think about what it means in general everyday contexts, and then in relation to the particular subject and to the literary methods of this novel.

Focus on: Nicola Six, and the Murderer, the Murderee and the foil

ASK YOURSELF . . .

— 'She outwrote me. Her story worked. And mine didn't. There's really nothing more to say' (p. 466). What does Sam mean? Who did murder Nicola? Is that what you expected? From the point of view of the novel's self-consciousness, how might this be an appropriate conclusion?

ENDPAPERS (pp. 468–70)

Focus on: Endpapers

CONSIDER . . .

— Why is this an appropriate title for the last section of the book? Why do you suppose Sam chooses these two particular people to write to – that is, Mark Asprey and Kim Talent?

RESEARCH, DESCRIBE AND ASSESS . . .

— On p. 469 Sam speaks about the poem called 'Strange Meeting' written by Wilfred Owen during the First World War. Try to find the poem and read it, and then describe what it is about and how that illuminates the themes of *London Fields*. Then assess the effectiveness of this reference in the light of the images of doubleness and the methods of repetition or doubling that have been played out in the novel.

Looking over Chapters 13–24

QUESTIONS FOR DISCUSSION OR ESSAYS

1. 'So in a way, everything goes back to darts. If you think about it, the whole world is darts' (p. 396). Make a case for the analogy between darts and the themes of this last twelve-chapter section of *London Fields*.

2. 'I failed, in art and love' (pp. 467, 469). Why is this Sam's confession?

Looking over the whole novel

QUESTIONS FOR DISCUSSION OR ESSAYS

1. 'Nicola Six is the true author of *London Fields*.' Argue for this proposition.

2. 'Readers have to work hard for Amis.' How? And why?

3. 'Christ, it's only just occurred to me: people are going to imagine that I actually sat down and made all this stuff up' (p. 302). Discuss.

4. Nicola considers winding Guy up with 'A few more choice ambiguities' (p. 341). How might this phrase stand in as a description of the novel as a whole?

5. Explain the importance of any *one* of the following characters to the plot or the themes of the novel: Incarnacion, Lizzyboo, Lady Barnaby, Missy Harter.

6. In *London Fields*, everything happens at least twice. Explain how Amis's literary methods and stylistic devices support the themes of the novel.

7. 'A hollow cosmic joke, that touches us all.' Is this a fair description of *London Fields*?

Contexts, comparisons and complementary readings

LONDON FIELDS

Focus on: true stories and postmodern games with fiction

EXAMINE . . .
— On p. 1 the narrator of *London Fields* tells us, 'This is a true story but I can't believe it's really happening.' What do you expect of a 'true story'? Is there ever such a thing as a story that is 'true'? Or will it always be – to some extent – a controlling and ordering of reality, and, therefore, 'false'?
— Look up 'postmodern' in a glossary of literary terms. Also look up 'fictionality'. How would you go about positioning the fictional method that Amis uses in *London Fields*? In what ways is it 'true'? In what ways is it fiction? In what ways does it go about confessing and acknowledging its own 'fictionality'?

RESEARCH AND COMPARE . . .
— Read Samuel Beckett's *Murphy* (1938). How does the narrative technique compare with Amis's? Or else read Jeanette

Winterson's *The Passion* (1987). It is also a love story and a murder story. How does that text point up its 'fictionality', and how does Winterson's method compare with Amis's?

ANALYSE DOUBLING TECHNIQUES . . .
— Many scenes in *London Fields* are repeated so that you have a double perspective on every event. If the counterpoint were another text – rather than just another take on the same scene – then the term for this would be 'intertextuality'. Nevertheless, the same devices of cross-reference and comparison are used. Read Tom Stoppard's play *Rosencrantz and Guildenstern are Dead* (1966) or his *Travesties* (1974). The first uses Shakespeare's *Hamlet* as its counterpoint background text, the second uses Oscar Wilde's play *The Importance of Being Earnest* (1895). How do the doubling techniques used by these plays compare with Amis's method?

Focus on: murder stories

RESEARCH AND COMPARE . . .
On p. 1 the narrator of *London Fields* tells us, 'It's a murder story, too.' The murder story is a form that has become extremely popular since the nineteenth century. Compare different types of murder stories. For instance, you might read a Sherlock Holmes short story such as Arthur Conan Doyle's 'The Speckled Band' or Agatha Christie's *Murder on the Orient Express* (1934), or Ruth Rendell's *A Dark Adapted Eye* (1986). What conventions do these stories set up, and in what ways does Amis's novel subvert and disrupt those conventions?

OR ELSE YOU MIGHT . . .
— Otherwise you could read Tom Stoppard's play *The Real Inspector Hound* (1968). This plays with both the genre of the

murder and detective story, and with literary notions of intertextuality and fictionality. Compare Stoppard's range of tricks
with Amis's.

Focus on: the theme of love

NOTE . . .

— On p. 1 the narrator of *London Fields* tells us, 'And a love
story (I think), of all strange things, so late in the century, so
late in the goddamned day.' What do you expect of a love
story? As the narrator is unsure, do you think that *London Fields*
is a love story?

— Apart from the beginning, there are several references to
love and what it might be (e.g., on pp. 440–1). Collect these
discussions and use them to think about Amis's treatment of
the theme of love.

RESEARCH AND COMPARE . . .

— See the film *Love Story* (1971) or read the book (1970) by
Erich Segal. What are the key elements that make this a 'love
story' and how do they compare with Amis's version?

— Or else read Jeanette Winterson's *Written on the Body* (1992).
Is that your idea of a 'love story'? What elements in Winterson's
novel might allow for a comparison with Amis's book?

— Or else read Roland Barthes's critical and analytical reverie
called *A Lover's Discourse: Fragments* (1977). How do Barthes's
quotations and references illuminate your idea of what 'love'
consists of and how it might be represented in literature? And
how does Barthes's perspective help you with Amis's?

Focus on: literary influence and allusion

RESEARCH AND ASSESS . . .

— Amis says that two writers whose work appeals to him are Vladimir Nabokov and Saul Bellow. In the course of *London Fields*, the narrative refers to works by Vladimir Nabokov (p. 303), Saul Bellow, Ernest Hemingway (p. 412), Jorge Luis Borges (p. 389) and James Joyce. Read any works by any of these writers and consider how their approaches to literary method and/or to certain themes and concepts might have influenced the text of *London Fields*.

Focus on: Hiroshima

CONSULT HISTORY . . .

— Read Leonard Cheshire's account of the events up to and around the bombing of Hiroshima and Nagasaki in *The Light of Many Suns: The Meaning of the Bomb* (Methuen, London, 1985), the book Nicola gives to Guy.

— How do either or both of these books help you to gauge Nicola's special and peculiar perversion of reference to this event?

Focus on: child abuse

THINK ABOUT WHAT YOU KNOW . . .

— Babies and children – because they are dependent, vulnerable and powerless – have always been mistreated or abused by some. Today, most people and most nations would agree that such behaviours towards children are morally corrupt and an infringement of human rights. How does the treatment meted out to Kim Talent compare with cases of child abuse that you have heard about or read about?

— Find out about the National Society for the Prevention of Cruelty to Children campaign called 'Stop' which seeks to track, prevent and mitigate the ill-treatment of children. You can find them at www.nspcc.org.uk.

— Ask yourself how you feel about Kath and her relation to Kim. Think also about her relation to Keith.

Focus on: second sight

COMPARE . . .

— Read George Eliot's novella called *The Lifted Veil* (1859). Her character Latimer – like Nicola Six – is able to see into the future. Compare the treatment of this subject in Eliot's novella with Amis's *London Fields*.

CONSIDER THE LITERARY ANALOGY . . .

— Look up the term 'omniscient narrator' in the glossary of literary terms. Think about its relevance and consider the proposition that Nicola herself is very like an omniscient narrator – because she too 'knows all' and can predict her own future, just as a novelist can predict the futures of his characters because he's the one who's going to write them.

— If you agree that Nicola is a variation on the 'omniscient narrator' theme, then consider the effect that this has on your attitudes to the text you are reading.

VINTAGE
LIVING
TEXTS

Time's Arrow

IN CLOSE-UP

Reading guides for

TIME'S ARROW

BEFORE YOU BEGIN TO READ . . .
— Read the interview with Amis. You will see there that he identifies a number of themes:

- Narrative structure and method
- History
- Political manipulation and moral choice
- The portrayal of atrocity
- Time and memory

Other themes that may be useful to consider while reading the novel include:

- Absence and presence

Reading activities: detailed analysis

TITLE

Amis recounts in the Foreword to *London Fields* (1989) that he considered calling that earlier novel *Time's Arrow*; when he came back to the title later it suggested other possibilities. What does the title *Time's Arrow* suggest to you? 'Arrow' suggests what? A sharp point (like the needle or hand on a dial)? Or something that travels fast, like a bullet, with an unequivocal path? A missile? A pointer, like a finger, perhaps in accusation? An emblem of love, like a pierced heart, or a broken heart?

CONTENTS

Look at the Contents page. Can you infer any of the themes of the novel from these headings? How many suggest cause and effect? How many suggest moral evaluation? How many suggest a value, whether emotional, moral or of some other kind?

PART I

1. WHAT GOES AROUND COMES AROUND
SECTION 1 (pp. 11–14)

Focus on: openings and narrative voice

INFER . . .
— What do you infer about the speaker in this opening section? This is a first-person narrative: the narrator is a character. The narrator's 'voice' – comprising the tone, the choice of words, the register, the habits of thought and expression – are therefore an integral part of the narrator's characterisation. How the narrator speaks should be 'read' as attentively as what s/he says.
— 'Given my circumstances' (p. 12). What seem to be the narrator's circumstances? What aspects are unexplained, contrary to expectations, confusing?

ANALYSE THE LANGUAGE . . .
— Look for words with associations of violence, death and sickness; then trace words of healing, life and health. What do you conclude about the way that these two word orders are combined in this opening?

PART I, CHAPTER I
SECTION 2 (pp. 14–24)

Focus on: setting

IDENTIFY AND ANALYSE . . .
— This section opens with a sketch of 'innocuous America'

(p. 14). Amis often uses a type of metaphor called 'synecdoche', whereby a part of something stands for the whole. Identify examples of synecdoche on pp. 14–15, and analyse the impressions you form of Tod Friendly's environment from these.

Focus on: reversal and dissociation

DISTINGUISH FRIENDLY'S REACTIONS . . .
— Friendly realises his life is running backwards. He feels dissociated from his environment, and from his own thoughts, from himself. Find the words and phrases that indicate his reactions to this bizarre state.

REFLECT AND DEFINE . . .
— The novel starts from a daring premise: time runs backwards. This reversal creates some amusing consequences. Consider eating a meal backwards, or blowing one's nose, or other functions of the body. How does this reversal make ordinary actions (like eating) revolting? Words take on their opposite meanings: 'buying' means 'selling', 'getting up' means 'going to bed'. What does 'friendly' become (though he *seems* friendly enough . . .)? It also throws our intuitions into disarray. How does memory work in reverse? Does effect lead to cause, and if so, does the process of getting younger entail becoming gradually more innocent – less knowing, and also less guilty? Does free will disappear? If Friendly is experiencing his life backwards, what was the oblivion out of which he emerged on p. 11? Who was the 'male shape, with an entirely unmanageable aura' (p. 12)? This conceit also raises some practical problems. How, for instance, is speech to be represented intelligibly?

Focus on: Tod Friendly and the narrative alter ego

EVALUATE . . .

— Evaluate Friendly's general knowledge (pp. 16–17) and the level of his reading (pp. 19–20). What is his attitude to these? Does the narrator share all of Friendly's opinions?

CONJECTURE AND DISCUSS . . .

— The final words of this chapter are 'exiled or demoted soul' (p. 24). There are references earlier to Friendly's fear, to his shame, to committing mutilation (e.g. p. 15), and to the narrator's disapproval of Friendly's behaviour. Discuss the possibility that the narrator is Friendly's soul, exiled by Friendly, and of which Friendly is unaware (p. 22).

Focus on: narrative strategy

REVIEW . . .

— Review the chapter headings on the Contents page. Now that you know the basic conceit behind the narrative strategy, what new meanings do these headings take on? And what of the novel's title, *Time's Arrow*?

Looking over Chapter 1

QUESTIONS FOR DISCUSSION OR ESSAYS

1. What impressions of Tod Friendly's social environment have you formed from Chapter 1?

2. Discuss the theme of dissociation, as it is developed in Chapter 1.

PART I

2. YOU HAVE TO BE CRUEL TO BE KIND
SECTION 1 (pp. 25–33)

Focus on: reversals

ANALYSE THE EFFECTS . . .

— 'Destruction – is difficult . . . Creation, as I said, is no trouble at all' (p. 26). Analyse the comic effects Amis creates to illustrate this idea on pp. 26–8.

— Read the conversation on pp. 28–9, first as it is written, then in reverse. The claim that Friendly changed his name and 'ran' ties in with references to guilt earlier in the narrative. This detail draws our attention to the irony that is alive throughout a reversed narrative: the reader must continually re-evaluate 'earlier' incidents in the face of 'later' events which throw light on them by explaining what caused them, and so put them in a clearer perspective.

Focus on: chaos and order

EXPLORE THE IMPLICATIONS . . .

— 'There are accidents, sure, and yet it all works out. The city streams and pours in this symphony of trust' (p. 30). These sentences present images of chaos giving way to order. What are the implications if the process is reversed?

— 'Words make plain sense' (p. 32). Explore the idea that this narrative is an exercise in making the 'plain' sense of words complicated.

Focus on: the process of 'youthing'

INTERPRET . . .

— Friendly moves out of a 'morally neutral' (p. 30) old age

into vigour, which the narrator associates with cruelty, 'which is bright-eyed, which is pink-tongued . . .' (p. 31). In what ways does this subversion of the cliché of the undesirable ageing process provoke a fresh perspective?

PART I, CHAPTER 2
SECTION 2 (pp. 33–56)

Focus on: irony

LOOK FOR EXAMPLES . . .
— The narrator observes Friendly's activities uncomprehendingly: an irony is set up between what he misunderstands and what the reader fully understands. This means that the reader can judge what the narrator cannot. Look over this section and find examples of this irony.

Focus on: power

CONNECT IDEAS AND EXPLORE . . .
— 'I was flooded by thoughts and feelings I'd never had before. To do with power' (p. 45). Look at earlier and later comments about power: 'The devil has something to be said for him: he acts on his own initiative and isn't just following orders' (p. 17); 'Sometimes [Friendly] glows with great power, which rushes out and solves and clears everything: a power lent by the tutelary maker who presides over all his sleep' (p. 37). About his dreams he says, 'I wish I had power, just power enough to avert my eyes' (p. 48). Explore the idea of power in this section.

DISCUSS . . .
— 'It seems to me that you need a lot of courage, or a lot of

something, to enter into others, into other people' (pp. 46–7). If it doesn't take courage, but something else, what is that 'something'?

Focus on: dreams

ANALYSE THE TENSION . . .
— The narrator has 'an intractable presentiment that I will soon start seeing . . . in Tod's dream' (p. 47), something about 'vanished' babies – something that 'Tod will eventually do' (and has therefore already done). In this order of reality, dreams that are for Friendly the crucible of memories are for the narrator nightmare premonitions of what will certainly happen. Analyse the effects of the tension between Friendly's understanding and the narrator's.
— Look at the description of Friendly's dream about babies on pp. 53–5. Analyse the way in which this episode brings together contrasting ideas.

Focus on: metaphor

INFER . . .
— What point is the narrator making about Friendly's 'central mistake about human bodies' (p. 48)?

ASK YOURSELF . . .
— On pp. 49–51, the narrator talks of Friendly's prejudice and confusion and danger. Then he describes the insane logic of the reversed world. Which is more confused?

Focus on: attitudes to women

ANALYSE . . .
— Analyse the attitudes to women expressed on pp. 55–6. Whose are they: Friendly's or the narrator's?

PART I, CHAPTER 2
SECTION 3 (pp. 57–73)

Focus on: context

RESEARCH CONTEXT . . .
— The narrative is set in 1970 at this point. Look up what was happening at that time in a chronicle of the twentieth century. What details has Amis selected, and what has he left out? What effects are created by the details he has included?

Focus on: irony

ANALYSE WITH CLOSE READING . . .
— Analyse what the passage on pp. 57–9 implies about identity and conscience, and analyse how it implies this.
— Analyse what the passages on pp. 59–63 and 65–6 convey about Friendly's motives for his relationships with women.

NOTE THE EXAMPLES . . .
— There are a number of details in this section which are not explained. They point forward ironically to events that gave rise to them and which will be explained later. Make a note of these details as they arise.

Looking over Chapter 2

QUESTIONS FOR DISCUSSION OR ESSAYS
1.   Evaluate the claim that, at this stage in the novel, the conceit of the reversal of time amounts to little more than ingenious wordplay.

2.   Analyse the narrative technique of Chapter 2 of *Time's Arrow*.

3.   What bearing does the title of this chapter have on the chapter itself?

4.   Comment on the relationship between Tod Friendly and the narrator.

PART I

3. BECAUSE I AM A HEALER, EVERYTHING I DO HEALS
SECTION 1 (pp. 74–86)

Focus on: the title

CONSIDER THE LOGIC . . .
— Consider for a moment the fallacious logic of the title: the second statement does not follow from the first. It only becomes logically correct if reversed: 'Because everything I do heals, I am a healer.' However, given that the acts of creation and destruction in this narrative are reversed, and Friendly's role as a doctor is to 'demolish the human body' (p. 83), the statement in the title takes on a sinister implication: 'Everything I do is justified by the labels I attach, to myself or others.' Which twentieth-century regimes used this argument to justify atrocities?

Focus on: identity and narrative strategy

CONSIDER AND LIST . . .
— 'Time, the human dimension, which makes us everything we are' (p. 76). What aspects of a person's life would you include in the idea of 'everything we are'? Make a list. How many of these things do we know about Friendly's life? Friendly

seems to have spent his time getting away from what he was, assuming new identities. Played in reverse, does the narrative of his life promise to lead through the layers of false identities – Tod Friendly, John Young – to his true identity? Or is the reader required to adopt an attitude of alert scepticism about every new 'fact' that we learn, in case this also is false? We cannot measure what we learn against what has happened so far in the narrative: we must wait to measure it against what is to come. How does this narrative strategy differ from the usual contract that exists between a novelist and a reader?

COMPARE . . .

— Compare the way that *Time's Arrow* subverts conventions of how fiction sets up identity with the way that Harold Pinter does this in his plays. Read *The Birthday Party* (1960), for instance, and examine how the information the audience is given about Stanley's identity is shifting and contradictory. What is his past? What does he do? Who is he? And what about Goldberg – what's his real name? Why does he seem to be continually reinventing himself? Pinter's technique questions the stability of the very idea of 'identity': it may be convenient for the audience to be told 'who' a character is, but this is a traditional cheat – how can anyone know who they are beyond borrowing a name, a role, a sense of race or nationality, or a set of beliefs? Might Amis be making a similar point?

ANALYSE WITH CLOSE READING . . .

— Analyse the techniques that the narrative employs to create the character of Kreditor.

Focus on: clues

DECIPHER . . .

— The narrative lays down a trail of clues about Friendly/

Young's past and about why he is on the run. Read carefully through the paragraph on p. 81 that starts '"The only present danger," Kreditor resumed'. What clues does the photograph, in the context of the conversation between the two men, give you about Friendly/Young's past? Consider the hideous inversion of what hospitals do on pp. 83, and think again of the title of this chapter.

PART I, CHAPTER 3
SECTION 2 (pp. 86–103)

Focus on: sex

SUMMARISE . . .
— Summarise what the narrative says about the connection between sex and power in Young's mind.

Focus on: memory and forgetting

TRACE . . .
— The narrator is surprised at the human capacity to forget (p. 89), but this only happens in reverse time of course. What hints have there been in the narrative so far that Friendly/Young finds it hard to forget his own past?
— If the narrator remembers the killing of JFK, President John F. Kennedy (p. 90), where can you place the narrative present at this stage in the novel?

Focus on: the theme of fear

REFLECT AND EXPLORE . . .
'Our hilarity contained terror . . . terror of our own fragility. Our own mutilation' (p. 93). Explore the link between fear and laughter in this section of the novel.

Focus on: hospitals

ANALYSE . . .
— How are hospitals represented in this section? How does the bizarre perspective of reversed time create surprising images and ideas about hospitals?

Focus on: addresser, addressee

COMMENT . . .
— 'All three of us know that John has a secret. Only one of us knows what that secret is' (p. 98). Comment on how the triangular relationship of narrator-character-reader works in this novel.

Focus on: parts of the body

COMPARE CONNOTATIONS OF IMAGES . . .
— What significances do 'heart', 'face', 'throat' and 'eye' have, with reference to the foetuses described on pp. 101–2? What significances have these images had earlier in Chapter 3, when referring to the women that Young pursues? Compare these two types of ideas.

Focus on: the limitations of language

EXPLORE THE LIMITATIONS OF LANGUAGE . . .
— What does 'atrocity' mean? What connotations does it carry that near-synonyms like 'violence', 'cruel act' or 'guilty act' (listed in a thesaurus) do not? Using a thesaurus, try to find a word that expresses an act of greater evil and cruelty than 'atrocity'. Does such a word exist in the English language? Can any word ever convey the extremity of an atrocity? Or is any attempt to label such an event always a euphemism, an acknowledgement of what it cannot express? Use a search facility to find references to atrocities in a national newspaper (you might

try http://www.guardian.co.uk or http://www.independent.co.uk or http://www.the-times.co.uk or http://CNN.com) and measure the events described against the language used to describe them.

Looking over Chapter 3

QUESTIONS FOR DISCUSSION OR ESSAYS

1. Discuss the significance of the human body throughout Chapter 3.

2. How has the theme of power been developed in Chapter 3?

3. Analyse the idea of 'soul' as it is presented in Chapter 3.

4. 'I keep expecting the world to make sense. It doesn't. It won't. Ever' (p. 91). How does *Time's Arrow* explore the ironies of this statement in Chapter 3?

PART II

4. YOU DO WHAT YOU DO BEST, NOT WHAT'S BEST TO DO
SECTION I (pp. 107–16)

Focus on: vigour

CONSIDER THE IMAGERY . . .
— 'His vigour, nowadays, contains something savage and tasteless. It is pink-tongued. It is feral' (p. 108). Look at earlier imagery that this echoes. 'John attends them both with his animal parts thickened' (p. 89); 'Cruelty, which is bright-eyed, which is pink-tongued' (p. 31). What ideas form around the

notion of 'vigour' in this novel? List them, and add to the list as you read on.

Focus on: names

COMPARE THE FAMILIAR AND THE EXOTIC . . .
— Tod Friendly and John Young are banal, familiar names. Hamilton de Souza is more exotic, and suggests to us that Friendly/Young/de Souza's roots might be less familiar than we had expected. Notice, though, that all three adopted names are unimaginative. Connect this idea with the way that de Souza is 'ever the literalist' (p. 108). In what ways has this characteristic of unimaginative literalism been present throughout his portrayal?

Focus on: locale

COMPARE THROUGH AN ANALYSIS OF IMAGERY . . .
— Compare the setting of the villa near Redondo with that of New York in the previous chapter.

Focus on: palindromes

RESEARCH AND CONSIDER . . .
— The narrator's claim that he can only understand *somos* (p. 112) continues the verbal playfulness with which Amis presents the reversal of time. It is a palindrome, because it reads the same backwards. The narrator has drawn our attention to this conceit as early as p. 16, when he lists 'palindrome' as an instance of his 'superb vocabulary'. What other palindromes can you think of?
— 'Deed' is the same, backwards and forwards – but is a deed?

126

Focus on: inferences

INFER . . .
— Performing a running reversal to 'make sense' of events
according to our time logic, we note that Hamilton de Souza
exchanges gold for money (p. 113). Put together the clues: the
date, the place, the fact that he will soon be on the run, the
reference to tooth solder. What connotations does gold have
in this context? What is it about the mood of these transac-
tions that supports your inference?

Focus on: sentimentality and psychosis

COMPARE . . .
— Compare the descriptions of Rosa and of the camp on
pp. 113–15 with de Souza's views of her. In what ways is his
sentimentality seen to be a substitute for genuine feeling? How
are images of the colour pink on pp. 113–15 used to suggest
that de Souza's reactions to Rosa are psychotic: that he cannot
see the girl herself, only the images into which he makes her?

PART II, CHAPTER 4
SECTION 2 (pp. 117–23)

Focus on: the crucified Christ

INTERPRET . . .
— How is it fitting that de Souza sees the crucified Christ
only as 'the worshipped corpse' (p. 118)?

Focus on: the perfecto

CONSIDER THE MOTIF . . .
— Friendly/Young/de Souza's 'perfectos' (cigars) are more

127

consistent than his identity. Note that they recur with the frequency of a leitmotif, each time with an alliterating adjective: 'a pensive perfecto' (p. 22); 'with plausible perfecto' (p. 107); 'one's penitent perfecto' (p. 120) are examples. Despite his changes of identity his character is in some ways consistent. An arrogant belief in his own superiority runs throughout, as does hedonism, as does a capacity for posing. How are these ideas conveyed by this recurring motif?

Focus on: guilt and penitence

ANALYSE IMPLICIT MOTIVES . . .

— Read de Souza's conversation with Father Duryea on pp. 120–1. What does he admit to? Is it a confession? Gauge how sincere de Souza is in expressing penitence. Assess the validity of the claim that 'You do what you do best [. . .] not what's best to do' (p. 120) as an excuse for his actions. What is he seeking?

ASSESS AND RESEARCH . . .

— Comment on the reactions of Father Duryea. Do you interpret his willingness to understand as a sign of Christian love? Of moral laziness? Does he compromise Christian ideals by his reactions to de Souza? You might research historical accounts of reactions of the Roman Catholic Church to Nazi atrocities by doing a web search on Pope Pius XII. According to John Cornwell, in *Hitler's Pope: The Secret History of Pius XII* (Penguin, London, 2000), the wartime Pope's 'silence' in the face of the Jewish genocide was tantamount to counterwitness to what was happening. For a rebuttal of this argument, you might go to http://www.beliefnet.com

— Analyse the language the narrator uses to describe Odilo Unverdorben's impressions of his '*charmed*' journey on pp. 121–2 (from 'And clean heels' to 'It never did anything'). What do you make of the personification of the land as clean-cut and innocent? The word 'painterly' draws attention to its symbolic qualities, and may recall the pictures of clean-cut Aryan farmers living close to the land of Nazi propaganda. Look for examples of such pictures. What do they say about Nazi ideals of purity, nature and national identity?

Looking over Chapter 4

QUESTIONS FOR DISCUSSION OR ESSAYS

1. 'Sentimentality is the false emotion of those who cannot feel.' Is this claim an accurate description of de Souza's expressions of emotion in Chapter 4?

2. Discuss the themes of innocence and guilt in Chapter 4.

3. What aspects of his attitude and outlook associate de Souza/Unverdorben with a Nazi mindset in this chapter?

4. 'I might be impressed and affected by this sudden talent for suffering, if it weren't for its monotony: fear, just fear, fear only' (p. 119). Consider the idea that de Souza cannot feel for anyone but himself.

PART II

5. HERE THERE IS NO WHY
SECTION I (pp. 124–35)

Focus on: the power of a name

EVALUATE YOUR RESPONSE . . .
— 'Auschwitz' is first mentioned on p. 124. How do you react to this name? What connotations does it carry?

RESEARCH AND PRESENT . . .
— What do you know of the real Auschwitz? Do some research. You might look at the Auschwitz museum at http://www.auschwitz-muzeum.oswiecim.pl/html/. If you are in a group, it might be useful to discuss and combine your knowledge.

ANALYSE . . .
— Analyse the sentence, 'Auschwitz lay around me . . . like a somersaulted Vatican' (p. 124). What other Roman Catholic images figure, and to what effect?
— What does 'preternatural purpose' (pp. 124, 127, 128) mean to the narrator? Linked to the title of this chapter, what does it mean to you?

Focus on: cross-references

CONNECT AND PREDICT . . .
— Connect the image of Unverdorben donning black boots and white coat with previous allusions to this image (e.g., pp. 12, 48, 72). Given these and other clues that have been trailed throughout the novel, predict what Unverdorben's crime has been.

Focus on: irony and knowledge

TRACE AND REACT . . .
— The inversion of Young's life as a doctor finds a shockingly dark counterpoint here. Trace the ironies on pp. 126–35, and gauge your reactions to them. These ironies depend on our having a greater knowledge of what is really happening than the narrator. In what sense does this technique highlight the collective human loss of innocence that the Holocaust brought about?

Focus on: beauty and ugliness

ANALYSE THE LANGUAGE . . .
— Look at the description of the doctor, 'Uncle Pepi', who was 'coldly beautiful, true, with self-delighted eyes; graceful, chasteningly graceful in his athletic authority' (p. 127). What ironic effects are created by these words in this context?

RECONCILE . . .
— Bearing the above in mind, can you reconcile the 'quest for greater elegance' (p. 128) among the guards at Auschwitz with what they do?

Focus on: coprocentricity

COMPARE . . .
— Why is there an emphasis on human faeces? Compare the focus on excrement in this chapter with that in Part IV of Swift's *Gulliver's Travels*, especially in Chapters VI and VII. Philip Pinkus, in *Sin and Satire in Swift* (1965), writes:

> Since Swift's constant concern in his satires is man's
> corruption from original innocence, there is no more
> graphic illustration than the excremental. That is why
> his satires are obsessed with it. It is the traditional
> imagery of evil, of which Swift's contemporaries
> were well aware [. . .] All Swift's references to the
> unclean flesh, the dung, the stench, the filth of
> man's body, are the symbols of man's sin.

Does excrement have a symbolic function here? If so, what does it symbolise?

PART II, CHAPTER 5
SECTION 2 (pp. 135–45)

Focus on: 'the bomb baby'

INTERPRET THE SYMBOL . . .

— The narrator has alluded throughout to the 'bomb baby' that exerts 'such power over its parents' (p. 135), and 'the mortal importance of no one knowing they are there' (p. 101). See also references to this idea on pp. 48, 55, 67. What does this dream image seem to symbolise? Make what sense of it you can. It will be more clearly explained later. What effects are created by these orders of unexplained images?

Focus on: insane perspectives

COMPARE . . .

— The narrator's inverted perspective has created a gap between what he says and what we understand. What he sees as creative magic, we know to be a delirious account of insane destruction. But when Herta confronts Unverdorben about ugly truths, the narrator's delusional system of thought goes into overdrive, using insane inversions to justify atrocities. He sees time backwards, of course, and cannot see straight: but by this stage, is there anything to distinguish the insanity of the narrator's inverted perspective from that of Unverdorben, or 'Uncle Pepi', or any of the others who inhabit the world of forward time and are guilty of the crimes that are described? Compare the delusional thought systems of the narrator and of his human counterpart, Unverdorben.

Focus on: 'Uncle Pepi'

COMMENT . . .

— What more do we learn about 'Uncle Pepi' in this section?

Consider in particular the details that frame his portrait on pp. 136 and 144–5.

RESEARCH . . .
— Research the historical figure of Josef Mengele. Is 'Uncle Pepi' a fictionalised portrait of this man?

PART II

6. MULTIPLY ZERO BY ZERO AND YOU STILL GET ZERO
SECTION I (pp. 146–52)

Focus on: character

APPRAISE . . .
— What impressions do you form of Unverdorben's life before 1942 from this section? Do any details surprise you? Which details help to explain his subsequent behaviour? In what ways does this portrait humanise him?

Focus on: memory

EXAMINE AND CONNECT . . .
— Read the episode on pp. 149–51 describing how Unverdorben discovered thirty Jewish 'souls' hiding, because a baby's cries gave them away. Which previous moments in the novel does this episode help to explain? Review the allusion on p. 101: what new significance does the phrase, 'the mortal importance of no one knowing they are there' take on in the light of this episode? Look again at p. 135: 'the physical power that the bomb baby exerted, over its parents and over everybody else in the black room: some thirty souls.' Given that the

explosive effect of the baby's cries was to betray them to Unverdorben, why does he dream about it so obsessively and threateningly? Remember that he has a child himself soon afterwards.

Focus on: 'time's arrow'

INTERPRET THE SYMBOL . . .
— The metaphor of time's arrow takes on a new significance on p. 151. Interpret what meanings it takes on here.

PART II, CHAPTER 6
SECTION 2 (pp. 153–6)

Focus on: despair

CONSIDER THE CLAIM . . .
— Unverdorben's soul regards him as a 'ruined god, betrayed and beaten by his own magic', and says that Unverdorben is 'on his own' (p. 156). We have seen the consequences of Unverdorben's soul dissociating from him at this moment. Consider the claim that Unverdorben's soul is portrayed as powerless, delirious and obtuse.

PART II

7. SHE LOVES ME, SHE LOVES ME NOT
SECTIONS 1 AND 2 (pp. 157–66)

Focus on: herd instinct

INTERPET THE TELLING DETAIL . . .
— 'individually we have no power or courage, but together we form a glowing mass' (p. 160). How does this passing comment about Unverdorben as a young man give the key to his later actions?

Focus on: qualified pastoral

PICK OUT THE DETAILS . . .
— The account of Unverdorben and Herta's courtship has a nostalgic atmosphere: partly because we know how he will degenerate afterwards, and partly because it draws on images of pastoral innocence. But the idyllic picture is complicated by the fact that Nazi ideology appealed to this nostalgia, this illusion of the purity of nature. What details in this apparently harmonious picture sound a dissonant note?

Focus on: impotence and power

ASSESS . . .
— In what ways does this section (especially pp. 161–6) suggest that Unverdorben's actions as an older man can largely be explained by his sense of sexual frustration, impotence and loneliness as a young man?

Focus on: the mother figure

CONSIDER . . .
— Unverdorben's life has been full of lovers; the passage on

pp. 165–6 offers the first explicit mention of his mother. What does this glimpse add to your understanding of Unverdorben?

PART III

8. BECAUSE DUCKS ARE FAT
SECTIONS 1 AND 2 (pp. 169–73)

Focus on: chickens and ducks

RELATE AN EPISODE TO THE WHOLE . . .
— In the chicken and duck story (p. 171), Unverdorben voices his inchoate ideas about distinctions: what does this anecdote reveal about his childish understanding of good and bad, and about what he has the right to decide? What is the significance of this episode?

Focus on: innocence and corruption

ASSESS THE CLAIM . . .
— 'He has to act while childhood is still here before somebody comes and takes it away. And they will come' (p. 173). Assess the validity of the claim that 'By finishing at the point of innocence, albeit temporary, Amis reasserts the value, after a story of the vilest degradation, of human goodness and potential.'

Focus on: the end

INTERPRET . . .
— What is the significance of the final arrow image on p. 173?

AFTERWORD

CONNECT . . .
— Look at the final paragraph of the Afterword, on p. 176. Do the ideas that Amis states explicitly here throw any light on ideas that have been implicit in the novel, especially in Part III?

Looking over the whole novel

QUESTIONS FOR DISCUSSION OR ESSAYS

1. Who, or what, is the narrator of *Time's Arrow*, and what is his relationship to the main character?

2. Consider and discuss the relationship between power and impotence in *Time's Arrow*.

3. Discuss the ways in which *Time's Arrow* presents the human body.

4. In your opinion, does the playful conceit of time running backwards make a coherent point about the human capacity for evil?

5. 'consciousness, or selfhood, or corporeality, is intolerable' (p. 78): 'Consciousness *isn't* intolerable. It is beautiful' (p. 82). Is either of these points of view supported by the novel?

6. Discuss the role of memory in the novel.

7. Explore the link between humour and terror in the novel.

8. What meanings does the title, *Time's Arrow*, take on in the novel?

9. 'One of the key concepts in Nazi ideology was that of 'progress': the narrative conceit of *Time's Arrow* can itself be seen as an ironic comment on that idea'. Discuss.

10. Consider the representation of women in the novel.

11. What importance does fear have in *Time's Arrow*?

Contexts, comparisons and complementary readings

TIME'S ARROW

Focus on: the theme of the 'Holocaust' or 'Shoah'

RESEARCH . . .

— Find out about the real events of the 'Holocaust'. Claude Lanzmann's film *Shoah* (1985) is a nine-hour documentary created out of a series of interviews with some 350 survivors and witnesses of concentration camps at Treblinka, Auschwitz, Sobibor, Chelmno and Belzec. It includes accounts by the people who assisted in the extermination: a Polish barber tells how he cut the hair of those about to go to the gas chamber; an SS officer talks about the 'processing' of the victims; a railway worker describes the practical difficulties associated with transporting so many Jews to the camps.

— Read Anne Frank's *Diary of a Young Girl* (1949). Anne was a teenage Dutch girl whose family, along with another Jewish family, managed to hide from the Nazis in an 'annexe' at the back of a house in Amsterdam. After some years, they were betrayed and deported, and Anne died in the camp at

Bergen-Belsen. Her father published her diaries after the war.
— Read the memoir by the Italian writer Primo Levi recollecting his experiences in the concentration camp at Auschwitz, *Se questo è un uomo* (*If this is a man*, 1947). You might also like to read the other books by Levi that Amis lists in his Afterword as being influential: *The Truce, The Drowned and the Saved* and *Moments of Reprieve*.
— Read Robert Jay Lifton's book *The Nazi Doctors: Medical Killing and the Psychology of Genocide* (1986), another text cited by Amis.

RESEARCH 'HOLOCAUST' STORIES ON FILM . . .

— A great number of films have been made about the concentration camps set up under the Nazi regime during the 1930s. Examples might include Steven Spielberg's *Schindler's List* (1993), Roberto Benigni's *La Vita è Bella* (*Life is Beautiful*, 1997), Alan J. Pakula's *Sophie's Choice* (1982) and Liliana Cavani's *Il Portiere di Notte* (*The Night Porter*, 1973). One such film that features a Nazi dentist who should be a healer – as in *Time's Arrow* – is John Schlesinger's *Marathon Man* (1976).
— Compare the filmic treatment of the facts of the concentration camps with Amis's literary treatment of the same subject.

VINTAGE
LIVING
TEXTS

Experience

IN CLOSE-UP

Reading guides for

EXPERIENCE

BEFORE YOU BEGIN TO READ . . .
— Read the interview with Amis. You will see there that he identifies a number of themes:

● Past, present, future
● The idea of the author
● Figurative language
● Fiction versus memoir
● Postmodernism
● Experience

Other themes that may be useful to consider while reading the memoir include:

● The literary treatment of violence
● Absence and presence
● Fathers and sons
● Fathers and daughters
● The author as reader

Reading activities: detailed analysis

THE TITLE

CONSIDER . . .

— Think about the meaning of the title. Amis discusses the idea of 'experience' in the interview on p. 25. Write down all the meanings that the word might convey to you.

THE CHAPTER HEADINGS

PLAY . . .

— Before you begin to read, just look over these chapter titles and the way they are set out, and let yourself imagine what they might contain. Jot down your thoughts to come back to later.

THE PICTURES

INTERPRET . . .

— If you looked at the pictures before you began to read, ask yourself why you did that. What were your motives? Did you also read the captions? How do you feel about the inclusion and selection of these pictures?

PART ONE: UNAWAKENED

INTRODUCTORY: MY MISSING
(pp. 3–11)

Focus on: literary structure

CONTEMPLATE THE METHOD . . .
— Consider the following extracts:

I have before me Julian Barnes's letter of 12 January
1995. Technically this piece of paper is my property,
but the text is Julian's copyright. I won't quote from
it, except to say that its last phrase is a well-known
colloquialism. That phrase consists of two words.
The words consist of seven letters. Three of them
are *f*s [p. 247].

That letter I wrote to Julian is his property but my
copyright [p. 248].

Experience is a story full of absences. Most crucially, in this particular passage, there is the absent phrase that we can easily
guess at. But there's also the untold – but implied – story of
a long friendship, and there's the untold – but understood –
breaking off of that friendship. And there's the absent letter,
that Amis does not quote, though he has the piece of paper
before him.
— There's another thing; the difference between property and
copyright, between what you can own and how. Note that Amis
does not contravene English law. He quotes his own letter –
as he is entitled to do, because it is his copyright. He does not
quote Julian Barnes's letter because, though the piece of paper
is his property, the copyright resides with Barnes.
— So there is a range of literary shapes in here. Absence

and presence, repetition, the gap between something said and not said. The beat of time that lets our own knowledge in, as we begin to understand. Note that these technical, rhythmic, structuring literary devices are paralleled by that contrast between the letter and the spirit, the said and the meant – the speech conveyed and the intention, the significance behind it.

— Now let's add two more key phrases: 'this wasn't the first time I had been close to an absence' (p. 53); and 'Children need a beat of time, to secure attention while the thought is framed' (p. 3).

ANALYSE WITH A CLOSE READING . . .

— Take a pencil and mark up your copy of the book, or else get a clean sheet of paper and make some notes. Look at pp. 3–8. Write down or mark up each time the scene or episode changes in these few pages. Here are some guides to help you, but you could refine them even further:

- A 'real' exchange between Martin Amis and his son Louis
- A 'fictional' exchange between Kingsley Amis and his son Martin taken from one of Kingsley's novels (via the 'beat of time' concept)
- A footnote on the source of the quotation
- In the footnote, Kingsley's gloss on how, in that novel, he took some events from life
- Martin's gloss on the dedication to the text mentioned in the footnote
- Martin's explanation about how that 'fiction' was rooted in the 'real'
- Martin's retrospect on those 'real' events
- Martin's switch from Kingsley in 1954 to himself in 1973/74 when he was about to be awarded a literary prize previously won by his father

- A 'real' exchange between Martin Amis and his son Louis
- A footnote about the concerns and penalties of fame
- A meditation – in the main body of the text – on writing and why Martin is now telling the story of his life i.e. a) because Dad is dead, b) because he wants to set the record straight, c) because it has been forced upon him by the late twentieth-century cult of celebrity
- A reverie on the 'missing' elements and on loss ... on how intercessionary figures are no longer present. Then a list of important absences: a teenage girl, a blonde toddler ... These are Amis's 'missing'

— Now think about a number of things:

- How are the connections made between one scene and another?
- What happens to time?
- How does Martin make himself and his own imagination bigger than Kingsley's?
- How are negatives used here? Lucy 'never posted the letter', she 'never boarded the bus' (p. 5). How do these negatives insist on the absences that relate to the theme of 'My Missing'?
- On p. 5 Amis says, 'I didn't notice, while writing this book (I only noticed while *reading* it for revision) ...' Consider the difference between writing and reading. How far is this a metaphor for 'a beat of time'?
- How far is all of this literary technique related to Amis's views on 'the novelist's addiction to seeing parallels and making connections' (p. 7)?

CONSIDER, RESEARCH AND COMPARE ...
— What does a term like 'missing' or 'the missing' mean to you? In what context is it used? Think about lost persons and

pets, think about wars and catastrophes where there are the dead and 'the missing'.

— Then think about the verb – as opposed to the noun made out of it. What does it mean to 'miss' somebody? How are the two notions connected?

— Set out the linguistic possibilities of the word. Is it a verb, 'to miss'? Or an adjective, 'my missing doll'? Or is it a noun, 'the missing and the lost'? How does each relate to the other?

Focus on: fathers and sons

ASSESS AND COMPARE . . .

— Consider all the fathers and sons in this section. How does each example relate to the other? Why does this memoir begin with the word 'Dad'? Think about other narratives where a son is saying to his father, 'Dad.' You might look at the Old Testament of the Bible where Adam – demanding knowledge – is essentially God's son; or you might look at the New Testament, where Christ questions God the Father. Or you might look at Milton's *Paradise Lost* where he undertakes to 'explain the ways of God to Man'. How do these references illuminate a) the themes, and b) the absence–presence structure of the memoir as a whole?

Focus on: 'letter from'

NOTE AND REMEMBER . . .

— Pp. 9–11 are given over to a letter which is purportedly a real unexpurgated letter written by the young Amis. Note that he employs a similar fictional strategy in *London Fields*, so that each chapter falls in two halves – one the 'novel' that the narrator is supposed to be writing, and the other the narrator-author's own commentary on how he is writing the novel and his real-life relations with the characters.

149

COMPARE YOUR OWN ATTITUDES . . .
— Look at young Amis's assessment of George Eliot's *Middlemarch* and his attitude to Jane Austen. Do you agree?

PART ONE

RANK
(pp. 12–21)

Focus on: patterns

ASSESS WHY . . .
— The title of this chapter is 'Rank'. When you have read it through, read it again and note down all the instances where some kind of hierarchy or order of class, style, superiority, is invoked. The first instance is at the beginning where Amis talks about his height.

COMPARE YOUR OWN ATTITUDES . . .
— Look at young Amis's assessment on p. 21 of the literature he is reading at school. Do you agree?

PART ONE

WOMEN AND LOVE – I
(pp. 22–38)

Focus on: the theme of father and son

EXPLAIN WHAT YOU HAVE LEARNED . . .
— In spite of the title of this chapter, the main focus is on the story of the relationship between Kingsley and Martin.

Pick out everything that you have learned about that relationship and try to discriminate the things which bring them closest together.

Focus on: literary language

CONNECT . . .
— The chapter begins with Kingsley telling Martin about 'false quantities' in prose (p. 22). It ends with Martin's footnote on 'litotes' and 'bathos' added to his schoolboy letter (p. 37). What connects these two episodes? Why are they relevant to the picture you are building of Martin Amis as a writer?

Focus on: women and sex

ASSESS . . .
— Assess what you have learned from this chapter about Kingsley's attitude to women and sex, and about Martin's attitude to women and sex.

Focus on: the theme of control

INTERPRET AND ASK YOURSELF . . .
On p. 36 Amis speaks about 'control' and how fiction gives control, 'And I have always been in love with that.' Bear this theme in mind as you read. Consider how much, and what kinds of 'control' are possible in fiction. And what about non-fiction? Can you control a memoir or an autobiography? Ask yourself what kind of a text this is, if Amis is 'in love with' exerting literary control.

PART ONE

LEARNING ABOUT TIME
(pp. 39–57)

Focus on: the theme of time

WRITE OUT A CHRONOLOGY . . .

— As you read over this chapter, write out a chronology of events as they have happened in real time. You will need to jump all over the place to collect the bits and pieces. Remember to include things like the fact that Lord David Cecil failed Kingsley's B.Litt. at Oxford (p. 39) and the fact that Robert Graves once visited Thomas Hardy (p. 41). You will have to guess at the dates for these, but that's fine. Remember that Hardy died in 1928 and that Graves was quite a bit older than Kingsley Amis. You could look up their dates in the *Oxford Companion to English Literature* if you want to get a bit closer to a correct chronology. Remember also to include things like the Norwegian translator of Amis's novel *The Information* being given an award for his work on that book (p. 46), and – of course – all Martin's reminiscences.

— When you have completed this exercise to your satisfaction, ask yourself how long a time span is covered here. And then ask yourself: what is the literary effect of chopping the chronology up as Amis has done? What kind of story would he have written if he'd put it in the proper order?

Focus on: the theme of teeth

MAKE A NOTE . . .

— On p. 48 we are told the story of Amis's visit to a dentist. Note down all the references to teeth that you find from now on. Keep thinking about the implications of this theme and the ways in which Amis employs this fact of his experience as a metaphor. You might also look at the interview (on pp. 17–18) where he speaks about the attitude to the body expressed in his novels and consider the relevance of that to this theme.

Focus on: Delilah Seale

MAKE A NOTE . . .
— On pp. 50–2 Amis tells the story of showing his mother the photograph of Delilah Seale. This photograph has already been mentioned (p. 8). From now on make a note of all the episodes and stories that involve Delilah, and consider how her story relates to the themes of the book as a whole.

Focus on: Lucy Partington

MAKE A NOTE . . .
— The fact of Lucy's disappearance is mentioned on pp. 53–4. From now on make a note of all the episodes and stories that involve Lucy, and consider how her story relates to the themes of the book as a whole.

Focus on: my missing

DESCRIBE . . .
— Describe how the three themes listed above connect to the opening idea of 'my missing'.

PART ONE

BUS STOP: 1994
(pp. 58–75)

Focus on: the theme of transfiguration

RESEARCH AND COMPARE . . .

— Look up the word 'transfiguration' in a dictionary, prefer-ably the *Oxford English Dictionary*. Then look at the passage on p. 62 where Amis speaks about 'weeping and swearing, cursing and sobbing'. Here, he gives two examples of such experience: David Partington's just after his sister failed to come home in 1973; and Robert Graves's reaction to the announcement of the Armistice at the end of the First World War. Then he says 'Cursing and sobbing and thinking of the dead: there ought to be a word for that. "Grieving" won't quite serve. This is something anterior. It is, I think, not a struggle to accept but a struggle to believe' (p. 62).

— On the next page (p. 63) he says, 'I had no idea that a cru-cially significant – a transfiguring – experience lay before me'. Consider how many 'transfiguring' scenes and moments there are in this memoir. Think about the differences between words like 'transfiguration', 'transformation' and 'translation'. Look them all up in a dictionary to collect as many meanings as you can. Why is 'transfiguration' such a meaningful word? In what ways do grief, loss, death, reconciliation and forgiveness 'trans-figure' us?

— Look ahead to p. 69 where Amis explains the nature of the 'transfiguring' experience of Lucy Partington's memorial service. Consider how these emotional experiences might relate to the 'literary catharsis' and 'dramatic catharsis' that Amis men-tions here. Look up these terms if you are not familiar with them.

Focus on: imagination and compassion

IMAGINE . . .
— On p. 66 Amis imagines how he would feel if any of his children were to suffer the undifferentiated cruelty that his cousin Lucy Partington suffered. How do you feel about this? Why might it be important for a writer like Amis to write about imagining these things? How important is it to social interaction in general for individuals to be able to imagine the sufferings of others and to behave in a compassionate way?

LOOK AHEAD . . .
— Look at p. 71 where Amis permits himself one sentence to describe his own 'verdict' on Fred West. Consider each of the words chosen here. Imagine for yourself what your own 'verdict' would be.

Focus on: allusion and reference

RESEARCH . . .
— The short section on pp. 70–3 is called 'The Onion, Memory'. It refers to the title of a poem by Craig Raine that Amis discusses briefly on pp. 71–2. Try to find a copy of this poem and compare the conclusions about memory in Raine's poem with those in Amis's memoir.

PART ONE

THE HANDS OF MIKE SZABATURA
(pp. 76–88)

Focus on: the theme of self-creation

SEARCH AND LIST . . .

— If you look through this chapter – which is largely about teeth – you will find a number of references to the mouth and what mouths do, and how the mouth helps to express and form our character through our actions. List the examples. Then you might want to quantify the 'crimes' that the mouth might commit, as well as listing the positive things that mouths can do.

SEARCH AGAIN . . .

— 'Oh, let other pens dwell on the symptoms of fear' (p. 83). This is a misquotation from the last chapter of Jane Austen's novel *Mansfield Park* (1814) where she actually says, 'Let other pens dwell on guilt and misery.' In what ways here is Martin Amis once again using his 'mouth'? Think about quotation, misquotation, ventriloquism, mimicking.

Focus on: euphemisms

REFLECT . . .

— There is a short passage about 'putting a lightbulb down the wastemaster' and 'visiting the bishop' in the footnote on p. 87. Amis's editor at Jonathan Cape wondered if the first were a euphemism for 'having a stiff drink'. How many absurd euphemisms do you know? What is their purpose? Which is the most extravagant you can think of? What kinds of activities are they usually designed to allude to (but not describe)? Can you think of any that make you laugh? Might euphemisms have any serious functions?

PART ONE

FAILURES OF TOLERANCE
(pp. 89–109)

Focus on: failures of tolerance

CONSIDER YOUR OWN REACTION . . .
— On pp. 93–5 Amis discusses his father's anti-Semitism and how he tried to combat that. This passage also includes an account of how Martin himself was accused of anti-Semitism in writing *Time's Arrow*. What do you think of Kingsley's attitudes, and of Martin's attitudes as explained here? If you have read *Time's Arrow*, what do you make of this accusation of 'anti-Semitism'?
— In what ways – in this chapter – is Kingsley Amis shown *not* to fail in tolerance?

Focus on: the theme of innocence and experience

CONSIDER AND ASSESS . . .
— Look at the exchange between Amis and his mother on p. 106. How can you relate this conversation to the theme of innocence and experience in the novel as a whole?

Focus on: literary allusion

ASSESS YOUR OWN IDEAS . . .
— Young Amis, in his letter on p. 109, gives his reactions to more of the literature that he is reading. Do you agree with his judgements?

PART ONE

HIM WHO IS, HIM WHO WAS!
(pp. 110–27)

Focus on: allusion and comparison

RESEARCH AND COMPARE . . .
— Read John Donne's poem 'A Nocturnall upon St Lucies day, Being the shortest day' which Amis refers to on p. 110. Consider how it relates to the themes of *Experience* as a whole.
— You might also like to read Amis's review of John Carey's book on Donne, which you can find in Amis's, *The War Against Cliché* (2001).
— Compare Amis's actual review of Carey's book with what he says about it here.

PART ONE

THE CITY AND THE VILLAGE
(pp. 128–51)

Focus on: social consideration

ASK YOURSELF . . .
— Read pp. 129–32. Should Amis have taken his grandmother to Debenhams rather than the Randolph?

Focus on: the theme of innocence and experience

INTERPRET . . .
— On pp. 133–5 there is a long passage about innocence and experience and what they mean. Look back at the interview

with Amis and consider how it relates to this passage. Think also about the specific areas being discussed here: nakedness, sexual knowledge, childhood, guilt, power. How do each of these ideas connect to the theme as it is worked out in the book as a whole?

CONSIDER . . .
— Read the footnote on pp. 139–40 where Amis speaks about the memoir written by Anna-Marie, Frederick West's daughter. Think about this story. Think also about the way that Amis ends this footnote. What do you think of his tone and manner of handling this difficult subject?

NOW ASSESS AND RECREATE . . .
— Look at the passage about how Philip and Martin found their father living with Elizabeth Jane Howard (pp. 144–5). Think about this episode. Whose side are you on? Rewrite the story of this episode from the point of view of Kingsley, or from the point of view of Elizabeth Jane.
— How does this change your perspective on the episode?
— How does this connect to the overall theme of innocence and experience?

PART ONE

THE PROBLEM OF REENTRY
(pp. 152–74)

Focus on: reentry into what?

ASK YOURSELF . . .
— As you read over this chapter, consider its title and assess its relevance to the situation described.

Focus on: the body

SEEK OUT AND ASSESS . . .

— There are several reveries on the body, on pain, on weeping, blushing and eating in this chapter. Look out for them and list the language and the narrative methods Amis uses to describe these experiences. How do these passages relate to the themes of the memoir as a whole?

PART ONE

PERMANENT SOUL
(pp. 175–94)

Focus on: the theme of autobiography and self-construction

CONSIDER . . .

— Amis speaks here about his own critical ideas on the development of the novel at a particular time and about his own relation to the American writer Saul Bellow. He also speaks about the ways in which he constructed himself as an author at the same time as constructing his own conception of his life and his choices in a way of life. Look particularly at the footnote on p. 177 where he notes that *Money* was published on the day he got married. How do his literary concerns and interests in the theme of autobiography connect to the self-conscious creation of his own choices in life?

Focus on: vocabulary and writing

NOTE DOWN AND LOOK UP . . .

— Look at the sentences that begin the second paragraph on p. 178: from 'Filial anxiety, I now perceive,' to 'the talent that bothered me'. Write down all the unusual words that Amis uses in this passage. Look up any you don't know in a dictionary. Are they always unusual in themselves, or is it the use of a surprising or inappropriate context that makes them appear unusual? As you go on reading, carry on noting down unusual words and consider the use of this extensive vocabulary. Remember also that this is a chapter dealing with substantial accounts of three writers: Martin Amis himself, Kingsley Amis and Saul Bellow.

RESEARCH . . .

— A great number of other writers are also mentioned in this chapter. If you haven't come across their work already, find out about them and what types of works they wrote. What kinds of writers does Amis seem to favour?

PART ONE

EXISTENCE STILL IS THE JOB
(pp. 195–213)

Focus on: partings and separations

EXAMINE . . .

— Look at pp. 198 and 199 of this chapter. You will see that Amis discerns a running theme of 'severances', 'sunderings', 'partings' and 'separations' (p. 198), 'discontinuities' and 'disappearances' (p. 199). Try to count up how many of these emotional, physical and practical break-ups (and breakdowns) you have encountered in the stories of the memoir so far. In what ways is this the major theme of the memoir? Remember that the first chapter was called 'My Missing'. Remember also that – as Amis says – Lucy had a 'beautiful but now sorrowful surname'. Think about it.

Focus on: writers and writerly language

LOOK BACK AND COMPARE . . .
— On p. 203 Amis considers the dictionary definition of the word 'lurid'. He then goes on to analyse the common use of certain adverbs like 'single-handedly'. If you look back at pp. 22–3, you will find that there too he expounds on his own, and his father's, relationship with and attitude to language, its use, abuse and misuse. Why do Kingsley and Martin share these concerns with language? Note down ten words that — in your opinion — sum up the special ways in which Amis uses language. Now think about your ten words in relation to some other contemporary writer that you have read — Ian McEwan, for instance, or Margaret Atwood. Would you assign the same words to a description of how they use language?

PART ONE

WOMEN AND LOVE – 2
(pp. 214–33)

Focus on: women and love

LOOK BACK AND COMPARE . . .
— At pp. 22–38 there is a chapter called 'Women and Love – 1'. Look back at that section and consider how this later chapter mimics and departs from the patterns set up there.

Focus on: vocabulary

CONSIDER THE WORD AND ITS IMPLICATIONS . . .
— 'Necrotic' is the word that Amis uses to describe his father's description of the house at Hadley Common where he lived

with Elizabeth Jane Howard (p. 218). Look up the meaning and derivation of the word in a dictionary. How many other words in this section and in this chapter might connect to this word? And how do all those words connect to the themes of the memoir as a whole?

Focus on: the theme of violence

ASSESS . . .

'Divorce "is an incredibly violent thing to happen to you",' says Kingsley (p. 221). Consider the presentation of the theme of different kinds of violence and assess their relation to each other as presented here.

PART ONE

FEASTS OF FRIENDS
(pp. 234–51)

Focus on: the theme of friendship

COMPARE . . .

'Friendship, as I see it, lies at the midpoint between these two stanzas. It is a mysterious power: you show your friend your weakness, and somehow you are both the stronger . . .' (p. 237). A large part of this chapter is taken up with discussing the long and intimate friendship that existed between Kingsley Amis and the poet Philip Larkin. Another large part (in terms of significance, if not number of words) is to do with the friendship between Amis and the writer Julian Barnes. Compare these two accounts of friendships. Note that Amis begins this reverie on friendship with a comparison between a sentimental poem and its undercutting parody.

163

PART ONE

THINKING WITH THE BLOOD
(pp. 252–72)

Focus on: love

CONSIDER . . .

— 'In filling out the pain schedule "the hardest items of all have to do with love"' (p. 256). Look over this chapter and assess the ways in which Amis thinks about love. Look particularly at pp. 256–7, the story about his Jewish girlfriend on pp. 264–5 and the conclusion of the chapter on p. 269. What images does this account of love build up across these episodes?

Focus on: jokes

RESEARCH AND COMPARE . . .

— Read Sigmund Freud's essay on 'Jokes and Their Relation to the Unconscious' (trans. James Strachey, 1960). Then think about this essay in relation to Amis's remarks about jokes on p. 268. How do jokes help to diffuse tense, embarrassing and despairing situations?

Looking over Part One, 'Unawakened'

QUESTIONS FOR DISCUSSION OR ESSAYS

1. *Experience* has been described as 'fractured', 'clogged' and 'tangled'. How would you describe Amis's literary method?

2. Describe and explain your own picture of the 'character' of Amis, as derived from your reading of the book so far.

3. Is *Experience* a palimpsest, a concordance, a thesaurus, a dictionary or an A to Z?

4. Why do you suppose the title of this first section of *Experience* is called 'Unawakened'?

PART TWO: THE MAIN EVENTS

DELILAH SEALE
(pp. 275–82)

Focus on: my missing

LOOK BACK AND COMPARE . . .
— The opening section of this memoir was called 'My Missing'. How does this first chapter of Part Two relate to that theme? Look over this chapter and consider in what ways Delilah was not 'missing'. Also think about how she is now not missed. If you look over the interview with Amis, you will see that he mentions on p. 23 the Maureen Freely criticism that he writes of on p. 280.

PART TWO

ONE LITTLE MORE HUG
(pp. 283–355)

Focus on: fathers and sons

CONSIDER AND NAME . . .
— Delilah's story in Part Two is relatively short and it is sweet: it ends with love and reconciliation. Kingsley's story is longer,

and though it also ends with love and reconciliation, it goes through a number of different layers of meaning and interpretation before it arrives at that happy conclusion. Work through the chapter and characterise each phase of the relationship between father and son as it is played out in these last few months as told in this section.

Focus on: buggering the reader about

LOOK UP AND COMPARE . . .
— If you look at the interview with Amis (on pp. 16–17), you will see that he speaks of the time when Kingsley read his novel called *Money* where there is a character called 'Martin Amis'. Kingsley complained about this, and objected to 'buggering the reader about'. On p. 290 you will find Kingsley complaining that he feels 'buggered about' by the setters of the *Independent* crossword puzzle. Martin Amis, on the other hand, does not mind doing this to readers. What kind of reader might be his ideal? What kinds of qualities or skills do you think that you need to have to be a good (patient? tolerant? optimistic?) reader of Amis's work?

PART TWO

THE MAGICS
(pp. 356–66)

Focus on: narrative patterns and 'the magics'

COMPARE AND RELATE . . .
— Look at p. 361 where Amis thinks about the writing of the memoir, as opposed to the writing of a fiction: 'My life, it seems to me, is ridiculously shapeless. I know what makes a

good narrative, and lives don't have much of that – pattern and balance, form, completion, commensurateness.' If you have read any of Amis's novels, consider how often he uses repetitions and revisions, juxtapositions and analogies to make patterns. Then consider how he uses these same techniques in this memoir. And then look at p. 365 where he discusses 'the magics', which is the given title of this chapter. How have the two magics, the 'white' one of birth and growth and the 'black' one of death, shaped and patterned this memoir?

POSTSCRIPT: POLAND, 1995
(pp. 367–71)

Focus on: the theme of atrocity

COMPARE . . .
— If you have not already done so, read Amis's novel *Time's Arrow*. How does this short section in *Experience* illuminate your reading of that novel? And how does this section illuminate the concerns of the memoir as a whole?

APPENDIX: THE BIOGRAPHER AND THE FOURTH ESTATE
(pp. 372–82)

Focus on: the theme of narrative control

LOOK BACK . . .
— Much earlier on in this memoir Amis worried about the fact that it is hard for a writer of a memoir to have any control over 'life'. By contrast, the role of the fiction writer is one that does (or seems to) give 'control'. What, in your opinion,

is the purpose of this Appendix? How does it relate to the themes of the memoir as a whole?

ADDENDUM: LETTER TO MY AUNT
(pp. 383–6)

Focus on: the haphazard

ASK YOURSELF . . .

— Why do you suppose that Amis chooses to end this memoir with a 'real'(?) letter? How does this letter differ from the other 'real' letters you have read in the memoir so far? In what ways is it similar? What do you make of the subjects referred to in the letter? How many of them relate to the major themes of the book, and how are they handled here? Why do you suppose the pictures of the children are included? What does that suggest? What message might those images convey as the memoir comes to an end? How do these pictures connect to, or comment on, the snapshots of Amis that are used as the back and front cover of the paperback Vintage edition of *Experience*?

Looking over the whole book

QUESTIONS FOR DISCUSSION OR ESSAYS

1. 'The present phase of Western literature is inescapably one of "higher autobiography", intensely self-inspecting ... No more stories: the author is increasingly committed to the private being' (Amis). Discuss, in relation to *Experience*.

2. 'Leaving aside the teeth, there is no perceptible theme or structure to this memoir.' Do you agree?

3. 'Other than Amis and his dentist, the only figures given any real prominence are the author's two fathers: Kingsley, his biological father, and Saul Bellow, his literary mentor. Amis's relationship with these two men is at the heart of this book.' How important to the book are these two characters, in your opinion?

4. Look at the beginning and the ending of *Experience*. Why does it end with a letter illustrated with family snapshots?

5. How would you characterise this work in terms of literary experimental writing?

6. How do you feel about the structural inclusion of Martin Amis's own teenage letters?

7. Pick out the methods and techniques Amis uses in terms of a) metaphors, and b) ordering and patterning.

8. Should artists speak about atrocity? How far should they imagine it, reinvent and (therefore) repeat it? Why should they do this?

9. Why is this work called *Experience*?

10. How persuaded are you by the use of the subjective viewpoint in here, and by the argument that subjectivity is all?

11. Ask yourself some questions about a) the heritage industry, and b) the cult of celebrity. What are either (or both) of these entities? What social climate promotes them? Are they useful or necessary? Or are they pernicious?

12. What is 'private life'? How much of it should be in public? When is it dirty linen? When is it art?

13. Consider Amis's views on prizes. What purposes do you feel/think/know that they serve? What criteria for literary prizes would you like to see?

Contexts, comparisons and complementary readings

EXPERIENCE

Focus on: innocence and experience

RESEARCH AND COMPARE . . .
— Read the poems in William Blake's *Songs of Innocence* (1789) and his *Songs of Experience* (1794). In many ways these are the expression of a Romantic opposition between innocence and experience. Given that Amis's own memoir is called *Experience*, how might Blake's work relate to that of Amis?

Focus on: the historical facts

RESEARCH THE LITERARY BACKGROUND . . .
— Read any of Kingsley Amis's novels. *Lucky Jim* (1954) or *Take a Girl Like You* (1960) are among his best known. Try to place these novels in the context of Kingsley's life as written up in Amis's memoir. Remember that one of the things that Martin and Kingsley shared was an interest in literary language.

Remember also that Kingsley began his career as a poet (publishing *Bright November* in 1947 and *A Frame of Mind* in 1953) and continued to write poetry which Martin read and criticised.

RESEARCH THE BIOGRAPHICAL BACKGROUND . . .

— Kingsley Amis's letters were published in 2000, in *The Letters of Kingsley Amis* edited by Zachary Leader. Read this volume or a selection of letters from it and assess how the facts of Kingsley's own life, as revealed in these letters, overlap with the focus employed by Martin in the memoir.

Focus on: literary influences

RESEARCH AND CONSIDER . . .

— Amis in the interview says that the two writers to whom he most directly relates as a reader are Saul Bellow and Vladimir Nabokov. Read any of their books – perhaps those mentioned in *Experience* – and consider the ways in which their style and treatment might have affected Amis in his own work. You might also like to look at Amis's collection of reviews and essays called *The War Against Cliché: Essays and Reviews 1971–2000* (2001). He writes there about Nabokov (pp. 245–63 and pp. 471–90) and about Bellow (pp. 323–27 and pp. 447–69).

RESEARCH AND CONSIDER . . .

— Although the poet Philip Larkin was Kingsley Amis's friend, rather than Martin's, several of Larkin's poems are quoted in the course of *Experience*. Find any such passage and look up the relevant poem to see how it fits in the context of the allusion. Or read some of Larkin's collections of poems, *The Whitsun Weddings* (1964) for instance, or *High Windows* (1974), and compare the tone and the sentiments expressed there to the passages where Amis mentions Larkin in *Experience*.

Focus on: memoirs

— Some of the earliest novels in English were written in the form of a 'memoir', that is, they purported to be the true auto-biographical history of their subject and often included diaries and letters, much as Amis includes many of his own letters in *Experience*. Such memoir-novels could include Daniel Defoe's *Robinson Crusoe* (1719), and *Moll Flanders* (1722). Can you think of any other famous novels which masquerade as 'memoirs' even though they are clearly fictional? Charlotte Brontë's *Jane Eyre* (1847), for instance, is subtitled 'an autobiography'.

— Given that fiction can be presented as a memoir, how far are memoirs fictional? In what ways might they be organised or presented along the same lines? If you look at the inter-view with Amis (on pp. 22–3) you will see that he agrees that some of the same principles apply as in the writing of a novel. Think about the overlap between fiction writing and memoir writing, and make three lists: one comprising the elements that are distinctively to do with the novel; one comprising the ele-ments that are distinctively to do with memoir and autobiog-raphy; and one where you include elements that might appear in either. How does this help you to define the differences between a memoir and a novel? Or does the comparison only further confuse the distinction?

VINTAGE LIVING
TEXTS

Reference

Selected extracts from reviews

These brief extracts from contemporary reviews of Amis's work are designed to be used to suggest angles on the text that may be relevant to the themes of the books, their settings, their literary methods, their historical contexts, or to indicate their relevance to issues, questions or problems today.

Sometimes one reviewer's opinion will be entirely contradicted by another's. You might use these passages to ask yourself whether or not you agree with the writer's assessments. Or else you may take phrases from these reviews to use for framing questions – for discussion, or for essays – about the texts.

The excerpts have been chosen because they offer useful and intelligent observations. Remember, though, two things about newspaper reviews: they are often written under pressure; and they have to give the reader some idea of what the book under discussion is like, so they do tend to give space to summarising the plot.

None of these critical opinions are the last word. They are simply contributions to a cultural debate. As such, they should be approached with intellectual interest – because they can give the mood and tone of a particular time – and they should be treated with caution – because the very fact of that prevailing mood and time may distort a clear reading.

Alan Taylor
From *Scotland on Sunday*, May 2000
On his literary tone

Amis, for all his egoism and narcissism, is a writer
of tremendous verve and appeal. He is the one
English writer with an American sense of ambition,
always, as it were, trying to outbellow Bellow, his
mentor. He ought to have been born American for
he would have been better appreciated.

Ian Hamilton
From the *Sunday Telegraph*, 21 May 2000
On literary techniques

[*Experience*] is described as a 'work of autobiography',
and so it is, but in truth it is more like a series of
cunningly juxtaposed snapshots. We are switched
backwards and forwards from the callow and super-
cocky young Martin of the early books to the new
battered-by-life 50-year-old.

There is a lot of remorse and recantation in this
book – a book, the author says, of sunderings and
breakages, of heart-rending losses and dizzying new
gains and a perhaps too-urgent need to exhibit some
transfiguration of the self.

Fans of the old – that is, the young – Martin
Amis will miss the essentially sardonic, unillusioned
world-view that used to power his jokes, although –
it should be said – there are more than a few
glimpses here of how things used to be. Journalists
and biographers get spat on now and then, and
there is an amusing commentary on the handful of

letters to Kingsley written by the 'drawling, velvet-suited, snakeskin-booted youth' of yesteryear.

On the whole, though, we are invited to welcome a changed Martin Amis: chastened, sage and heartfelt, a grown-up who has learned – from life as well as from Saul Bellow – that 'you need heartbreak to keep you human' . . .

There is . . . a perhaps excessive craftiness in the construction of the book, its flashbacks, cross-connections, inter-weavings, and so on. Thus, we can jump from an early reference to John Donne 'gritting his teeth' to Donne's 'Nocturnall for St Lucies Day' to Lucy Partington, and back to gritted teeth and Martin's dentistry, with side-reflections on light versus dark, innocence versus experience, and so on. It's ingeniously done, and the technique recurs throughout, but ingenuity and gravitas don't always mix too well.

David Sexton
From the *Glasgow Sunday Herald*, 28 May 2000
On literary control and style

In the past, Amis has announced that non-fiction necessarily lacks 'moral imagination, moral artistry'. 'The trouble with life (the novelist will feel) is its amorphousness, its ridiculous fluidity. Look at it: thinly plotted, largely themeless, sentimental, and ineluctably trite.' At another point in this memoir he says of Saul Bellow's many marriages: 'But that's life. We all have lives. It was the writing that excited me.'

Amis has always believed quite simply that it is the novelist's privilege to control life, to give it form, as no other man can. It's a god-like state, in his homespun theology. Throughout this memoir he still pointedly distinguishes between 'novelists' and lesser beings. Most of Amis's fiction has revolved around the question: who is the novelist here?

Now he is coming to understand that he cannot, after all, exert full control, not even in his novels. 'Even fiction is uncontrollable. You may think you control it. You don't.' And life is worse.

When his father dies, a friend says, 'It's like losing a part of yourself, isn't it?' Amis muses: 'Yes, that is exactly what it was like. And you know you're dealing with experience, with main-event experience, when a cliché grips you with all its original power.' For the first time in this book Amis appreciates that clichés are not the weakest part of speech. For the man whose mission has always been not to write a sentence that any guy could have written, this is a big change.

Douglas Kennedy
From the *Dublin Sunday Tribune*, 28 May 2000
On style

One of the first great surprises (and pleasures) of *Experience* is its structural brilliance. Refusing to follow chronological sequence, brimming with vast footnotes and annotations, the book really does read like a guided tour through Amis's mental and emotional baggage. Amis – always the most cunning of stylists – has devised *Experience* as a sort of reflection of his thought processes. As such, it is fragmentary, non-linear, but wholly gripping. Not only does he prove himself to be a tough arbiter of his own life, but he also demonstrates something that has been sorely lacking from his previous works: a true emotional core.

Unlike his fiction – with its explosive pyrotechnics, its cutting-edge prose, and its cartoonish characters – *Experience* grapples with that most human of dilemmas: the way we fail others and ourselves.

Christopher Wood
From the *Times Higher Education Supplement*, 18 August 2000
On words

Martin ... is happy to describe himself as a 'prose stylist' and his autobiography, *Experience*, provides ample evidence of what he means. Just as one of his novels begins 'I am a police' [*Night Train*], *Experience* contains an abundance of odd usages, starting with the first chapter title, 'My Missing', where a noun is at least one thing that is missing. Synonymic repetition is another (Martin) Amis hallmark, as when he ruminates after his dad has taken a fall: 'There were the slow and majestic subsidences ... And there were other types of trips, tumbles and purlers.' One can faintly hear the Roget he has swallowed swirling around uncomfortably as it refuses to go down.

James Wood
From the *Guardian Weekly*, June 2000
On genre and literary time

Experience is not quite a memoir, nor is it quite a
portrait of his father, Kingsley, nor is it really an
autobiography. It is an escape from memoir; indeed,
an escape into privacy. In the very book that may, at
first glance, seem exhibitionist, most shamelessly
metropolitan, Amis has retreated to the provinces of
himself. The book often reads like a letter to his
family and closest friends. It is sometimes embarrassing to read; the ordinary reader feels voyeuristic,
but very moved. What seems at first just gossip and
guest lists – sprays of names offered without
explanation, diaristic footnotes, a refusal to univer-
salise – becomes a tender defiance, as if Amis
wanted the book to vibrate with an atmosphere of
wounded privacy.

Thus *Experience* has an undulating, open-ended
form, something like a notebook whose pagination
has been erased. Chronology is scrambled, so that
we may move from the mid-90s back to Amis's
earliest childhood, forward to the 70s, then forward to the moment at which he is writing the
book.

Experience reminds us that life is lived backwards
but is thought forwards. We are always thinking for-
wardly – what next? – yet more often than not what
comes next has already been decided by the court of
our past, so we must live backwardly. Amis's book is
imbued with this sense of the past, especially childhood, as a future already determined.

One such determinism – it is the book's main

theme – is that innocence will necessarily become experience, song turn to growl.

Victoria Glendinning
From the *Daily Telegraph*, 30 May 2000
On form, method and genre

Form, Martin writes, comes from a novelist's addiction to seeing . . . parallels and making connections.

That is how this book works, and indeed it is how memory works. One thing leads to another, generally to fear and death, otherwise to tooth trouble and sex. Thus the middle-aged Martin's embarrassment at buying Steradent in a chemist's is linked, by a circuitous route, with Kingsley's buying his teenage sons a celebratory gross of condoms, having learned that they would put them to good use.

Amis approvingly quotes Julian Barnes as saying that novelists do not write 'about' their themes and subjects but 'around' them. His first section – a long and winding road from innocence to experience – proceeds like a movie, in flashbacks and fast-forwards, the main themes dropped in with the casual menace of rattling chains, and the backstories gradually revealed, all exactly the kind of 'compulsive self-circlings' that Amis identifies in the 'higher autobiography' which he thinks literary fiction has become.

The narrative is punctuated by his letters home from school and Oxford (flowered shirts and crushed-velvet flares). Amis, by the way, has kept almost no letters, and none at all from his father –

183

the only clue here for anyone seeking evidence of oedipal destructiveness.

John Nash
From the *Sunday Business Post*, 4 June 2000
On genre, themes and voice

Originally subtitled 'A memoir' (the phrase was subsequently dropped), Martin Amis's new book is less the autobiography it has been called and more a book about death. More accurately, it is a book about living with death (be it 'natural' death, murder or suicide), about watching a loved one die, about grief and about missing . . .

It would be wrong to read this book as a novel, although it is constructed with Amis's customary intricate patterning and bravura style. One of the interesting points about this book for fans of the younger Amis's fiction lies in how he writes in the first person, seriously and at length, without the fictional outlet of throwing his voice into some disreputable character.

His work, after all, is at its most powerful when not only satirising the moral squalor of urban England and the United States, but also when ventriloquising the speech of his targets. Dialogue that takes its energy from painful mimicry is a skill inherited from the father. In *Experience* Martin Amis writes in his own voice but there is plenty of scope for the novelist's craft.

Craig Brown,
From *The Literary Review*, May 2000
On compassion and humour

The memoir of his father contained in *Experience* is, I think, a masterpiece. Up until now Martin Amis's weakness has been his lack of empathy with his subjects, so that, beneath all the amazing verbal pyrotechnics, his acute ear for yobspeak, his avaricious eye for human detritus, his portentous seriously-though warnings about nuclear winters, and so on, it has been possible to condense his artistic outlook into three words: 'Count me out.' But in writing about his father, it is as though he had managed to escape the trap of his solipsism to become his own father.

Here, for instance, is Martin's description of Kingsley picking up a newspaper crossword in hospital, not long before his death: 'I watched him: the compression of the lips, slightly vexed and put-upon; the emphatic exhalation through the nose; the preparatory wag of the head, as it settled down to reluctant concentration.'

This is observation sharpened by love. 'When he made you laugh, he sometimes made you laugh – not continuously, but punctually – for the rest of your life,' he writes, and his descriptions of his father are often blissfully funny.

Val Hennessey
From the *Daily Mail*, 18 May 2000
On period setting and humour

His descriptions of the Seventies – 'It amazes me
that any of us managed to write a word of sense
during the whole decade considering we were all evidently stupid enough to wear flares . . .', the dagger-
collared flower shirts, crushed-velvet loons,
'dust-furred' bed-sits, girls and dope – are wonder-
fully entertaining, as are his recollections of adoles-
cence (he failed A-level English), his complex about
the size of his bum, his lack of height, his peri-
patetic education and so forth.

Glossary of literary terms

Allusion A reference, explicit or implicit, in a work of literature to a person, time, place, thing, event, or to another literary quotation or text.

Analogy When one thing is measured or compared by reference to another thing, usually something similar.

Authorial commentary When the author – as opposed to the narrator – of a literary text steps in to comment on events or characters in the novel or poem itself. An example might be the authorial voice in W. M. Thackeray's *Vanity Fair* (1847–8) who takes it upon himself to criticise his own characters. More recently, John Fowles's *The French Lieutenant's Woman* (1969) includes the voice of an 'author' who comments on his own fiction.

Autobiography The story – or biography – of a person's life, told by the subject themselves.

Bathos Deriving from the Greek word for 'depth' and signifying the opposite of the 'sublime' which deals with 'loftiness' or high-flown sentiments or concepts.

Caricature Particular aspects of a character are exaggerated or in some other dramatic way distorted to bring out key elements in that character but in a manner that is larger than life.

Chronology The strict time-bound order of events, or else of a departure from that linear pattern of the record of events.

Cliché From the French term for a stereotype in printing – a nineteenth-century mechanical invention which meant that many copies of exactly the same text could be printed off. 'My better half', 'it never rains but it pours', 'beautifully written' are all clichés.

Colloquial The ordinary language of the everyday.

Comedy of manners A stylised form which might satirise, but certainly relies on, social conventions of whatever kind for its sources and its amusement value. Many Restoration comedies, such as Oliver Goldsmith's *She Stoops to Conquer* (1773), are comedies of manners, but so is Oscar Wilde's *The Importance of Being Earnest* (1895) and so are many popular television series such as *Are You Being Served?*

Conceit Originally, any concept or image – which is how it is often used in this book – but often suggesting a comparison between two things or situations that are apparently dissimilar. For example, John Donne's likening his and his mistress's love to a pair of compasses in the poem 'A Valediction: Forbidding Mourning'.

Delayed disclosure Putting off revealing some fact or key piece of information in order to build suspense.

Double entendre From the French, 'double understanding'. A double meaning, neither one cancelled out by the other. Most often relating to some erotic situation: 'Let me feel your purse.'

Double perspective When two points of view are given simultaneously or consecutively.

Dream narrative A story told in or about a dream. A narrative method often used by medieval writers, as in Geoffrey Chaucer's *The Book of the Duchess*.

Episode A scene or sequence of events. Sometimes an 'episode' in a novel may be played out and returned to several times over, in the memories of the characters for example, so that the 'episode' refers not just to the actual facts as they happened, but also to any reference back to those facts.

Euphemism Coining a phrase that means something different, more polite, than the thing to which it actually refers. In *Experience*, for instance, Martin Amis tells the story of how his father was asked if he wished to 'wash his hands'. 'No thank you,' he replied, 'I washed them behind a bush on the way down.' No hands were ever washed of course.

Extended metaphor When an image or comparison is carried on in different guises across a paragraph, a chapter or a book.

Fictionality Where a fiction announces itself as fiction in a self-conscious way, drawing our attention to that fact. For instance, the beginning of George Eliot's 'realist' text *Adam Bede* (1859) announces itself as fiction with the words 'With this drop of ink at the end of my pen I will show you . . .'.

Figurative language The literary language which is designed to do more than merely convey instructions or communicate information.

First person 'I' as opposed to 'you' (second person) or 'he' (third person).

Gloss From the word for 'tongue', but it has come to mean 'to explain' or 'to put a certain interpretation upon'.

Hamartia From the Greek 'error of judgement'. Sometimes translated as the 'tragic flaw', it is the key decision or characteristic weakness that leads to the downfall of the tragic protagonist.

Interior monologue The rendering of one's thoughts as they occur to yourself inside your own head. Willy Russell's play *Shirley Valentine* is almost entirely conducted as an 'interior monologue'.

Intertextuality When one literary text plays upon, parodies or repeatedly alludes to another literary text or to some set of scenes or events.

Ironic effect See J. A. K. Thompson, *Irony: A Historical Introduction* (1926). Irony is introduced whenever something is not quite what it seems and we learn that it is not what it seems. Essentially, two things are in opposition or react on each other, or undercut each other.

Leitmotif A recurring image or theme.

Literal According to the letter, according to the real facts.

Litotes From the Greek for 'plain', it suggests an understatement, usually where an affirmative is couched in terms of a negative. 'She's no Marilyn Monroe', meaning she's not attractive.

Memoir A record – personal and subjective – of the events and persons in someone's life.

Metaphor Where a word or idea which is commonplace in one situation is translated for use in another to make a form of identity as opposed to a comparison. 'My love is a red rose' is a metaphor. 'My love is like a red rose' is a simile.

Modernist Applied to the group of writers and artists working just up to, around, and after the First World War. Their work was distinguished by a propensity to break up old structures, to experiment with form, and their themes are typically exile, the city, the development of the psyche and the fluidity of time.

Narrative strategy The narrative plans which aspire to create a particular effect in the prose or plot, or an effect on the reader.

Narrative structure The shape or patterning of a narrative.

Objective correlative A phrase coined by T. S. Eliot in his essay 'Hamlet and his Problems' (1919): 'The only way of expressing emotion in the form of art is by finding an "objective correlative"; in other words, a set of objects, a situation, a chain of events which shall be the formula of that *particular* emotion.' The point is to trigger the same emotion in the reader by exploiting this comparison. Of course, this will always be dependent on the circumstances and the reactions of the reader in question.

Omniscient narrator When a narrator appears to 'know everything' including all the thoughts and motives of the characters.

Oral tradition Stories and poems passed on by word of mouth as opposed to by writing.

Palindrome A word or a number or a sentence that reads the same backwards as forwards: 'noon', for instance.

Parody The intentional 'sending up' or ridiculing of a particular work, image or theme, through a mimesis which is designed to undermine the original.

Pastoral Theocritus (*c*.308–*c*.240 BC) was the original writer of 'pastoral' lyrics. The term derives from the Latin word for shepherd but is generally applied to any kind of country life and is epitomised in the urban poet's longing for rural scenes of simplicity and innocence.

Pathos From the Greek for 'feeling' and originally meaning deep emotion in general, but now usually applied to feelings of tenderness, pity or sorrow.

Persona The literary term for the construction of the identity of a person or character in a fictional work.

Postmodernism The movement – though never named as such by those who practise it – that comes after modernism, and which is usually characterised by an excessive self-consciousness, self-aware literary experimentation and a fragmentation of form.

Puns When a word sounds the same as another word which

means something different. When a twelve-pound baby is born late: 'He was certainly worth the wait (weight).'

Reliable narrator Someone who is telling the story and who you can trust.

Romanticism An overall term for a style of writing in the late eighteenth century and early nineteenth century. It is characterised by a love of democracy, an emphasis on nature, experimentation with literary forms, allusion to earlier literary models (especially Greek and Roman models), a concern for the lofty or the 'sublime' and an interest in the exotic and the Gothic. The term was not invented by the contemporary practitioners themselves, but applied to them in the late nineteenth century.

Satire The literary art of making a subject ridiculous in order to make a political or socio-political point through the use of scorn, ridicule, indignation or extravagant language.

Stylising effect When something is given an artificial form, as opposed to one that is natural.

Symbolise When one thing represents, or is made to stand in for another. The wedding ring symbolises the fact of marriage.

Synecdoche From the Greek, 'taking together'. Where a part of something is used to signify the whole, as in 'the Crown' meaning the institution of monarchy.

Tabula rasa From the Latin, a blank page.

Third person 'He', as opposed to 'I' (first person) or 'you' (second person).

Tone In narrative, an implied attitude, like a 'tone of voice'.

Tragic flaw The key failure of personality which undermines the tragic hero and leads to his downfall.

Typology Originally referring to a method of reading the Bible begun by St Paul. All the events and persons in the Old Testament were perceived as, on the one hand, real in themselves, but at the same time, images which pre-figure or look forward to events and persons in the New Testament.

Unreliable narrator Someone who is telling the story and whom you can't trust.

Wordplay Games with words, whether to do with meanings, spellings or contexts.

Biographical outline

1949 25 August: Martin Louis Amis born. The son of Kingsley Amis and Hilary Bardwell.

1971 Graduated from Exeter College, Oxford, with a BA (hons) first class in English.

1972 Appointed Editorial Assistant at the *Times Literary Supplement*.

1973 *The Rachel Papers* published.

1974 Appointed Fiction and Poetry Editor at the *Times Literary Supplement*.

1974 Won the Somerset Maugham Award for *The Rachel Papers*.

1975 *Dead Babies* published. Appointed Assistant Literary Editor at the *New Statesman*.

1977 Appointed Literary Editor at the *New Statesman*.

1978 *Success* published.

1980 Film *Saturn 3*, written by Amis, released.

1981 *Other People* published.

1982 *Invasion of the Space Invaders* published.

1984 *Money* published.

1986 *The Moronic Inferno and Other Visits to America* published.

1987 *Einstein's Monsters* published.

1989 *London Fields* published. Film of *The Rachel Papers* released.

1991 *Time's Arrow* published. Shortlisted for the Booker Prize for *Time's Arrow*.

1993 *Visiting Mrs Nabokov and Other Excursions* published.

1994 *Two Stories* published.

1995 *The Information* published.

1997 *Night Train* published.

1998 *Heavy Water* published.

2000 *Experience* published. Won the James Tait Black Memorial Prize for Biography for *Experience*.

2001 *The War Against Cliché* published. Won the National Book Critics Circle Award for Criticism.

2002 *Koba the Dread* published.

Select bibliography

WORKS BY MARTIN AMIS

The Rachel Papers (Jonathan Cape, London, 1973; Vintage, 2003)

Dead Babies (Jonathan Cape, London, 1975; Penguin, 1984)

'My Oxford' in Ann Thwaite ed., *My Oxford* (Robson, London, 1977)

Success (Jonathan Cape, 1978; Penguin, 1985)

Other People: A Mystery Story (Jonathan Cape, 1981; Vintage, 1999)

Invasion of the Space Invaders, with an introduction by Steven Spielberg (Hutchinson, London, 1982)

Money (Jonathan Cape, 1984; Penguin, 1986)

The Moronic Inferno and Other Visits to America (Jonathan Cape, 1986; Penguin, 1987)

Einstein's Monsters (Jonathan Cape, 1987; Vintage 1999)

London Fields (Jonathan Cape, 1989; Vintage, 1999)

Time's Arrow (Jonathan Cape, 1991; Vintage, 2003)

Visiting Mrs Nabokov and Other Excursions (Jonathan Cape, 1993; Penguin, 1994)

The Information (HarperCollins, London, 1995)

Night Train (Jonathan Cape, 1997; Vintage, 1998)

Heavy Water and other stories (Jonathan Cape, 1998; Vintage 1999)

Experience (Jonathan Cape, 2000; Vintage, 2001)

The War Against Cliché (Jonathan Cape, 2001; Vintage, 2002)

Koba the Dread (Jonathan Cape, 2002; Vintage, 2003)

INTERVIEWS

'What I miss is ringing Kingsley to check on a language point.' Interview with Valerie Grove, *The Times*, 4 August 1997.

Interview with Andrew Billen, *Evening Standard*, 30 September 1998.

'England is great. But America has real chaos, and that's what writers like.' Interview with Deborah Orr, *Independent*, 19 May 2000.

WEBSITE

There is a website at http://martinamis.albion.edu set up by James Diedrick. It offers bibliographies and critical reading and links to sites where you can hear interviews with Amis.

CRITICAL WORKS

Saul Bellow, *The Adventures of Augie March by Saul Bellow*, with an introduction by Martin Amis (Everyman's Library, London, 1995).

Patrick Brantlinger, *Fictions of State: Culture and Credit in Britain, 1694–1994* (Cornell University Press, Ithaca, New York and London, 1996). Includes a discussion of Amis's *Money*.

James Diedvick, *Understanding Martin Amis* ed. Matthew Joseph Diedvick (University of South Carolina Press, Columbia S.C., c. 1995).

Greg Harris, 'Men Giving Birth to New World Orders: Martin Amis's *Time's Arrow*', in *Studies in the Novel*, Vol. 31, Part 4 (Winter, 1999), pp. 489–505.

Gerald Howard, 'Slouching towards Grubnet: The Author in the Age of Publicity' in Sven Birkets, ed., *Tolstoy's Dictaphone: Technology and the Muse* (Graywold, St Paul's Minneapolis, 1996), pp. 16–27.

Clive James, *Peregrine Prykke's Pilgrimage Through the London Literary World, a Tragedy in Heroic Couplets* (New Review, London, 1974).

Phil Joffe, 'Martin Amis's *Time's Arrow* and Christopher Hope's

Serenity House: After Such Transgressions, What Reconciliation?' in Hermann Wittenberg and Loes Nas, eds, *AUETSA 96, I–II: Southern African Studies* (University of Western Cape Press, Bellville, South Africa, 1996), I, pp. 200–12.

Dermot McCarthy, 'The Limits of Irony: The Chronological World of Martin Amis's *Time's Arrow*', in *War, Literature and the Arts: An International Journal of the Humanities* Vol. 11, Part 1 (Spring–Summer, 1999), pp. 294–320.

Jan Marta, 'Postmodernizing the Literature-and-Medicine Canon: Self-Conscious Narration, Unruly Texts, and the *Viae Ruptae* of Narrative Medicine' in *Literature and Medicine*, Vol. 16, Part I (Spring, 1997), pp. 43–69.

Richard Menke, 'Narrative Reversals and the Thermodynamics of History in Martin Amis's *Time's Arrow*' in *Modern Fiction Studies*, Vol. 44, Part 4 (Winter, 1998), pp. 959–80.

Joe Moran, 'Artists and Verbal Mechanics: Martin Amis's *The Information*' in *Critique: Studies in Contemporary Fiction*, Vol. 41, Part 4 (Summer, 2000), pp. 307–17.

Michel Morel, '*Time's Arrow*: ou, le recit palindrome', in Marie-Françoise Cachin et Ann Grieve, eds, *Jeux d'ecriture: Le Roman britannique contemporain* (Institut d'Etudes Anglophones, Université de Paris VII, Denis Diderot, Paris, 1995), pp. 45–61.

Ann Parry, 'The Caesura of the Holocaust in Martin Amis's *Time's Arrow* and Bernard Schlink's *The Reader*' in *Journal of European Studies*, 29 (3 [115]) (September, 1999), pp. 249–67.

David Rees, *Bruce Chatwin, Martin Amis and Julian Barnes: A Bibliography of their First Editions* (Colophon Press, London, 1992).

Kiernan Ryan, 'Sex, Violence and Complicity: Martin Amis and Ian McEwan' in Rod Mengham, ed., *An Introduction to Contemporary Fiction: International Writing in English Since 1970* (Polity Press, Cambridge, 1999), pp. 203–18.

Peter Stokes, 'Martin Amis and the Postmodern Suicide:

Tracing the Postnuclear Narrative at the Fin de Millennium' in *Critique: Studies in Contemporary Fiction*, Vol. 38, Part 4 (Summer, 1997), pp. 300–11.

Nicolas Tredell, ed., *The Fiction of Martin Amis* (Icon, Duxford, 2000).